D0078095

Sexual Offender Treatment: Biopsychosocial Perspectives

Sexual Offender Treatment: Biopsychosocial Perspectives has been co-published simultaneously as *Journal of Psychology & Human Sexuality*, Volume 11, Number 3 2000.

The *Journal of Psychology & Human Sexuality* Monographic "Separates"

Below is a list of "separates," which in serials librarianship means a special issue simultaneously published as a special journal issue or double-issue *and* as a "separate" hardbound monograph. (This is a format which we also call a "DocuSerial.")

"Separates" are published because specialized libraries or professionals may wish to purchase a specific thematic issue by itself in a format which can be separately cataloged and shelved, as opposed to purchasing the journal on an on-going basis. Faculty members may also more easily consider a "separate" for classroom adoption.

"Separates" are carefully classified separately with the major book jobbers so that the journal tie-in can be noted on new book order slips to avoid duplicate purchasing.

You may wish to visit Haworth's website at . . .

http://www.haworthpressinc.com

. . . to search our online catalog for complete tables of contents of these separates and related publications.

You may also call 1-800-HAWORTH (outside US/Canada: 607-722-5857), or Fax 1-800-895-0582 (outside US/Canada: 607-771-0012), or e-mail at:

getinfo@haworthpressinc.com

Sexual Offender Treatment: Biopsychosocial Perspectives, edited by Eli Coleman, PhD, and Michael Miner, PhD (Vol. 11, No. 3, 2000).

New International Directions in HIV Prevention for Gay and Bisexual Men, edited by Michael T. Wright, LICSW, B. R. Simon Rosser, PhD, MPH, and Onno de Zwart, MA (Vol. 10, No. 3/4, 1998). *"Performs a great service to HIV prevention research and health promotion. . . . It takes the words of gay and bisexual men seriously by locating men's sexual practice in their love relationships and casual sex encounters and examines their responses to HIV." (Susan Kippax, Associate Professor and Director, National Center in HIV Social Research, School of Behavioral Sciences, Macquarie University, New South Wales, Australia)*

Sexuality Education in Postsecondary and Professional Training Settings, edited by James W. Maddock (Vol. 9, No. 3/4, 1997). *"A diverse group of contributors–all experienced sexuality educators–offer summary information, critical commentary, thoughtful analysis, and projections of future trends in sexuality education in postsecondary settings. . . . The chapters present valuable resources, ranging from historical references to contemporary websites." (Adolescence)*

Sexual Coercion in Dating Relationships, edited by E. Sandra Byers and Lucia F. O'Sullivan (Vol. 8, No. 1/2, 1996). *"Tackles a big issue with the best tools presently available to social and health scientists. . . . Perhaps the most remarkable thing about these excellent chapters is the thread of optimism that remains despite the depressing topic. Each author. . . chips away at oppression and acknowledges the strength of women who have experienced sexual coercion while struggling to eliminate sexist assumptions that deny women sexual autonomy and pleasure." (Namoi B. McCormick, PhD, Professor, Department of Psychology, State University of New York at Plattsburgh)*

HIV/AIDS and Sexuality, edited by Michael W. Ross (Vol. 7, No. 1/2, 1995). *"An entire volume on the topic of HIV and sexuality, bringing together a number of essays and studies, which cover a wide range of relevant issues. It really is a relief to finally read some research and thoughts about sexual functioning and satisfaction in HIV-positive persons." (Associate of Lesbian and Gay Psychologists)*

Gender Dysphoria: Interdisciplinary Approaches in Clinical Management, edited by Walter O. Bockting and Eli Coleman (Vol. 5, No. 4, 1993). *"A useful modern summary of the State-of-the-art endocrine and psychiatric approach to this important problem." (Stephen B. Levine, MD, Clinical Professor of Psychiatry, School of Medicine, Case Western Reserve University; Co-Director, Center for Marital and Sexual Health)*

Sexual Transmission of HIV Infection: Risk Reduction, Trauma, and Adaptation, edited by Lena Nilsson Schönnesson, PhD (Vol. 5, No. 1/2, 1992). *"This is an essential title for understanding how AIDS and HIV are perceived and treated in modern America." (The Bookwatch)*

John Money: A Tribute, edited by Eli Coleman (Vol. 4, No. 2, 1991). *"Original, provocative, and breaks new ground." (Science Books & Films)*

Sexual Offender Treatment: Biopsychosocial Perspectives

Eli Coleman, PhD
Michael Miner, PhD
Editors

Sexual Offender Treatment: Biopsychosocial Perspectives has been co-published simultaneously as *Journal of Psychology & Human Sexuality*, Volume 11, Number 3 2000.

The Haworth Press, Inc.
New York • London • Oxford

Sexual Offender Treatment: Biopsychosocial Perspectives has also been published as *Journal of Psychology & Human Sexuality* Volume 11, Number 3 2000.

© 2000 by The Haworth Press, Inc. All rights reserved. No part of this work may be reproduced or utilized in any form or by any means, electronic or mechanical, including photocopying, microfilm and recording, or by any information storage and retrieval system, without permission in writing from the publisher. Printed in the United States of America.

The development, preparation, and publication of this work has been undertaken with great care. However, the publisher, employees, editors, and agents of The Haworth Press and all imprints of The Haworth Press, Inc., including The Haworth Medical Press and Pharmaceutical Products Press, are not responsible for any errors contained herein or for consequences that may ensue from use of materials or information contained in this work. Opinions expressed by the author(s) are not necessarily those of The Haworth Press, Inc.

Cover design by Thomas J. Mayshock Jr.

The Haworth Press, Inc., 10 Alice Street, Binghamton, NY 13904-1580 USA

Library of Congress Cataloging-in-Publication Data

Sexual offender treatment: biopsychosocial perspectives / Eli Coleman and Michael Miner, editors.
    p. cm.
    "Sexual offender treatment: biopsychosocial perspectives has also been co-published simultaneously as Journal of psychology & human sexuality, volume 11, number 3 2000"
    Includes bibliographical references and index.
    ISBN 0-7890-1017-8 (alk. paper) -- ISBN 0-7890-1018-6 (alk. paper)
    1. Sex offenders--Rehabilitation. 2. Sex offenders--Psychology. 3. Sex offenders--Physiology. 4. Brain--Abnormalities. I. Coleman, Eli. II. Miner, Michael, Ph.D. III. Journal of psychology & human sexuality.
RC560.S47 S496 2000
364.15'3--dc21
                                                                              00-036965

INDEXING & ABSTRACTING

Contributions to this publication are selectively indexed or abstracted in print, electronic, online, or CD-ROM version(s) of the reference tools and information services listed below. This list is current as of the copyright date of this publication. See the end of this section for additional notes.

- *Biology Digest*
- *BUBL Information Service An Internet-based Information Service for the UK higher education community <URL:http://bubl.ac.uk/>*
- *Cambridge Scientific Abstracts*
- *CNPIEC Reference Guide: Chinese National Directory of Foreign Periodicals*
- *Educational Administration Abstracts (EAA)*
- *Family Studies Database (online and CD/ROM)*
- *Family Violence & Sexual Assault Bulletin*
- *FINDEX <www.publist.com>*
- *GenderWatch*
- *Higher Education Abstracts, providing the latest in research & theory in more than 140 major topics*
- *IBZ International Bibliography of Periodical Literature*
- *Index to Periodical Articles Related to Law*
- *Mental Health Abstracts (online through DIALOG)*
- *Periodica Islamica*
- *Psychological Abstracts (PsycINFO)*
- *Referativnyi Zhurnal (Abstracts Journal of the All-Russian Institute of Scientific and Technical Information)*
- *Sage Family Studies Abstracts (SFSA)*
- *Sage Urban Studies Abstracts (SUSA)*

(continued)

- *Social Services Abstracts <www.csa.com>*
- *Social Work Abstracts*
- *Sociological Abstracts <http://www.csa.com>*
- *Studies on Women Abstracts*
- *Violence and Abuse Abstracts: A Review of Current Literature on Interpersonal Violence (VAA)*

Special Bibliographic Notes related to special journal issues (separates) and indexing/abstracting:

- indexing/abstracting services in this list will also cover material in any "separate" that is co-published simultaneously with Haworth's special thematic journal issue or DocuSerial. Indexing/abstracting usually covers material at the article/chapter level.
- monographic co-editions are intended for either non-subscribers or libraries which intend to purchase a second copy for their circulating collections.
- monographic co-editions are reported to all jobbers/wholesalers/approval plans. The source journal is listed as the "series" to assist the prevention of duplicate purchasing in the same manner utilized for books-in-series.
- to facilitate user/access services all indexing/abstracting services are encouraged to utilize the co-indexing entry note indicated at the bottom of the first page of each article/chapter/contribution.
- this is intended to assist a library user of any reference tool (whether print, electronic, online, or CD-ROM) to locate the monographic version if the library has purchased this version but not a subscription to the source journal.
- individual articles/chapters in any Haworth publication are also available through the Haworth Document Delivery Service (HDDS).

Sexual Offender Treatment: Biopsychosocial Perspectives

CONTENTS

Introduction: Promoting Sexual Offender Treatment Around
the World   1
Eli Coleman, PhD
Michael Miner, PhD

Standards of Care for the Treatment of Adult Sex Offenders   11
Eli Coleman, PhD
S. Margretta Dwyer, MA
Gene Abel, MD
Wolfgang Berner, MD
James Breiling, PhD
Reinhard Eher, MD
Jan Hindman, MA
Ron Langevin, PhD
Thore Langfeldt, PhD
Michael Miner, PhD
Friedemann Pfäfflin, MD
Peter Weiss, PhD

The Psychoneuroendocrinology of (Sexual) Aggression   19
Ritsaert Lieverse, MD
Louis J. G. Gooren, MD
Johanna Assies, MD

Social Information Processed Self-Perceived Aggression
  in Relation to Brain Abnormalities in a Sample
  of Incarcerated Sexual Offenders   37
    Reinhard Eher, MD
    Martin Aigner, MD
    Stefan Fruehwald, MD
    Patrick Frottier, MD
    Christine Gruenhut, MD

Self-Concepts and Interpersonal Perceptions of Sexual Offenders
  in Relation to Brain Abnormalities   49
    Stefan Fruehwald, MD
    Reinhard Eher, MD
    Patrick Frottier , MD
    Martin Aigner, MD

Brain Abnormalities and Violent Behavior   57
    Martin Aigner, MD
    Reinhard Eher, MD
    S. Fruehwald, MD
    Patrick Frottier, MD
    K. Gutierrez-Lobos, MD
    S. Margretta Dwyer, PhD

The Treatment of Adult Male Child Molesters Through Group
  Family Intervention   65
    Dorothy W. Walker, MS

Adult and Adolescent Female Sex Offenders: Experiences
  Compared to Other Female and Male Sex Offenders   75
    L. C. Miccio-Fonseca, PhD

RESPECT™: A 7 Step System to Treat Pedophiles Who Are
  Mentally Retarded, Have Mental Illness,
  and Physical Handicaps   89
    Thomas P. Keating, MA, LCSW, RT

Index   115

ABOUT THE EDITORS

Eli Coleman, PhD, is Director of the Program in Human Sexuality in the Department of Family Practice and Community Health at the University of Minnesota Medical School in Minneapolis, Minnesota. He is the author of numerous articles and books on the topics of sexual orientation, compulsive sexual behavior, gender dysphoria, chemical dependency and family intimacy, and the psychological and pharmacological treatment of a variety of sexual dysfunctions and disorders. Dr. Coleman has edited two books on the topic of sexual offenders: *Sex Offender Treatment: Psychological and Medical Approaches* (1982, The Haworth Press, Inc.) and *Sex Offender Treatment: Interpersonal Violence, Intrapsychic Conflict, and Biological Dysfunction* (1996, The Haworth Press, Inc.). Particularly noted for his research on pharmacotherapy in the treatment of compulsive sexual behavior and paraphilias, Dr. Coleman is past president of the Society for the Scientific Study of Sexuality. In addition, he is the founding and current editor of *Journal of Psychology & Human Sexuality* and *International Journal of Transgenderism* and serves as president of the World Association for Sexology (1997-2001) and the Harry Benjamin International Gender Dysphoria Association (2000-2003).

Michael Miner, PhD, is Assistant Professor and Psychologist in the Department of Family Practice and Community Health at the Medical School of the University of Minnesota at Minneapolis, where he directs sex offender treatment services in the Human Sexuality Program. Dr. Miner has been involved with sex offender treatment and research since 1986, first serving as the research psychologist for California's Sex Offender Treatment and Evaluation Project. The editor of *The Forum*, the newsletter for the Association for the Treatment of Sexual Abusers, he has written numerous papers and book chapters on relapse prevention with sex offenders, sex offender treatment outcome, and forensic and sex offender assessment. Dr. Miner's current research focuses on the evaluation of sex offender treatment and the empirical investigation of causal factors for child sexual abuse in adolescents and adults.

ALL HAWORTH BOOKS AND JOURNALS
ARE PRINTED ON CERTIFIED
ACID-FREE PAPER

Introduction:
Promoting Sexual Offender Treatment
Around the World

Eli Coleman, PhD
Michael Miner, PhD

SUMMARY. The authors give an overview of recent research in the field of sexual offender treatment which was presented at the 5th International Conference on the Treatment of Sexual Offenders in 1998 in Caracas, Venezuela. They introduce the recently revised Standards of Care for the Treatment of Sexual Offenders and the formation of a new International Association for the Treatment of Sexual Offenders. The authors conclude with recommendations for future research in this area. *[Article copies available for a fee from The Haworth Document Delivery Service: 1-800-342-9678. E-mail address: getinfo@haworthpressinc.com <Website: http://www.haworthpressinc.com>]*

KEYWORDS. Sex offender research, sex offender treatment, sexual offenders, standards of care

This volume contains selected papers from the 5th International Conference on the Treatment of Sexual Offenders that was held in

Eli Coleman and Michael Miner, are members of the faculty, Program in Human Sexuality, Department of Family Practice and Community Health, University of Minnesota Medical School, 1300 South 2nd Street, Suite 180, Minneapolis, MN 55454. Dr. Coleman was the Scientific Program Chair of the 5th International Conference on the Treatment of Sexual Offenders and Dr. Miner was one of the Scientific Committee Members.

[Haworth co-indexing entry note]: "Introduction: Promoting Sexual Offender Treatment Around the World" Coleman, Eli, and Michael Miner. Co-published simultaneously in *Journal of Psychology & Human Sexuality* (The Haworth Press, Inc.) Vol. 11, No. 3, 2000, pp. 1-9; and: *Sexual Offender Treatment: Biopsychosocial Perspectives* (ed: Eli Coleman, and Michael Miner) The Haworth Press, Inc., 2000, pp. 1-9. Single or multiple copies of this article are available for a fee from The Haworth Document Delivery Service [1-800-342-9678, 9:00 a.m. - 5:00 p.m. (EST). E-mail address: getinfo@haworthpressinc.com].

© 2000 by The Haworth Press, Inc. All rights reserved.

conjunction with Violencia 98 in Carcacas, Venezuela, March 22-27, 1998. We hope that this volume will help promote the increasing need for effective sexual offender treatment and rigorous scientific investigation around the world. We think the various works should help guide clinicians to develop state of the art treatment for sexual offenders based upon good theoretical conceptualization and outcome evaluation research.

Ironically, as we gain better understanding of the sexual offender and develop better treatment techniques, public policy around the world encourages more punishing laws and less support for treatment. With the greater awareness of the extent of sexual violence which is perpetrated against individuals, one can understand the outcry for punishment for the individuals and wanting all sexual criminals off the street for fear of further victimization. However, we know that punishment and incarceration does relatively little to stem the tide of rising sexual violence. Societies must face a very pragmatic decision: will it support therapeutic rehabilitation for individuals who have committed sexual crimes or will it succumb to public pressures to build more prisons and dole out longer sentences for their crimes?

We hope that by presenting these studies, that not only will sexual offender treatment be enhanced, but that public policy might be modified to support the development of effective treatment programs throughout the world.

At the 5th International Congress on the Treatment of Sexual Offenders (ICTSO), several important events occurred. First, there was a revision of the Standards of Care for the Treatment of Adult Sexual Offenders (Coleman, Dwyer, Abel, Berner, Breiling, Hindman, Honey-Knopp, Langevin, and Phafflin, 1996). The revised version is published as the lead article of this volume. We hope that this document helps in the support for the promotion of more effective treatment programs for sexual offenders. Previous versions have been useful to many people to challenge governments to establish state of the art programs and to ensure that sexual offenders are given the most professional and ethical treatment in the hopes of improving treatment outcome. We consider these Standards to be minimal standards that all treatment providers around the world should adhere to and believe that they are complementary and supportive of other published standards of care (e.g., The Association for the Treatment of Sexual Abusers,

1997). Further revisions of these standards will be made as advances in research call for changes in treatment principles or methodology.

The next important event, and perhaps one which may have the most long lasting effects, was the establishment of the International Association for the Treatment of Sexual Offenders (IATSO) on March 24th, 1998. After the Program in Human Sexuality at the University of Minnesota Medical School co-sponsored the first five international conferences beginning in 1989, there appeared to be consensus that a new international organization should be formed which would take primary responsibility for the continuity of these conferences in the future, updating the Standards of Care and insuring international representation.

IATSO is an international non-profit organization committed to the promotion of research of and treatment for sexual offenders throughout the world. IATSO is committed to advocating for humane, dignified, compassionate, ethical and effective treatment of sex offenders.

IATSO has the following goals and values:

1. Furthering the knowledge about the nature of sexual offenders and sexual offenses and the improvement of treatment methods.
2. Supporting the development and improvement of effective sexual offender treatment.
3. Committed to scientifically evaluating therapeutic methods and to periodically revising and disseminating the IATSO Standards of Care for the Treatment of Sexual Offenders.
4. Committed to scientifically evaluating studies of treatment effectiveness of sexual offenders.
5. Believes that sexual offender treatment and research is enhanced through international communication and exchange of ideas, research and treatment methods.
6. Believes that sex offender treatment should be widely promoted, available and accessible.
7. Believes that sex offender treatment will result in the reduction of the incidence of sex offenses.
8. Believes that punishment alone for sexual crimes is an inadequate deterrent for sexual crimes.
9. Believes that sex offender recidivism is reduced best by the treatment of the sex offender.
10. Believes that sexual offender treatment is a basic human right.

11. Believes that freedom from sexual aggression and sexual abuse is a basic human right.

IATSO intends to sponsor the biennial International Conferences on the Treatment of Sexual Offenders for the dissemination of new research, treatment methods and to provide continuing education and networking opportunities. It will also promote international, regional and local conferences on the treatment of sexual offenders. An important task for the association will be to update the IATSO Standards of Care consistent with advances in knowledge of the treatment of sexual offenders. In addition, the association will advocate for humane, dignified, comprehensive, ethical and effective treatment of sexual offenders throughout the world.

The papers contained in this volume represent some of the best and most important work presented at the conference. They reflect the general trend of developing greater understanding of biomedical correlates of sexual aggression, greater understanding of brain abnormalities, especially associated with violent sexual behavior, and to understanding the psychosocial correlatates to brain functioning. The papers included in this volume present further advances in understanding the complexity of sexual offender treatment, especially the importance of family interventions, and the issues of special populations including females, mentally retarded, and physically handicapped offenders.

One of the major advances is the greater understanding of psychoneuroendocrinology of sexual aggression. In the past, we have had very over simplistic notions of the role of hormones on sexual aggression leading to anti-androgen treatment as the main biomedical intervention. But as Ritsaert Lieverse, Louis Gooren and Johanna Assies point out, the role of androgens have been difficult to substantiate. They propose that aggression may be more related to a maladaptive stress response–one which is "ill-balanced" and potentially stemming from congenital factors or the effects of early childhood negative experiences. Aggression may result more as a function of an inappropriate and exaggerated response to a perceived threat than of elevated testosterone levels. These findings have important implications and suggest a different approach to psychotherapy emphasizing stress reduction and different pharmacological approaches to treatment other than anti-androgen treatment. This thesis is consistent with the more recent research supporting the use of other pharmacotherapies such as the use of selective serotonin reuptake inhibitors. They suggest that sexual aggressors may need a "re-tuning" of their stress response system through these types of pharmacological interventions and that psychotherapeutic interventions may need to focus more directly on emotional response and cognitive mediations of such responses.

The next paper in this volume also emphasizes the potential role of biomedical mechanisms, in particular, brain abnormalities which were found associated with incarcerated sexual offenders who tended to have engaged in more violent sexual behavior and had associated general impulsive and aggressive lifestyles. Through magnetic resonance tomography, the team of Reinhard Eher, Martin Aigner, Stefan Fruehwald, Patrick Frottier, and Christine Gruenhut at the Department of Social Psychiatry at Vienna University Medical School were able to detect brain abnormalities in those with the most violent histories compared to those with less violent histories. Those with brain abnormalities were found to exhibit differences in processing social cues and emotions. The implication of this study is that the lack of empathy, callousness, and manipulations associated with the more violent and recalcitrant sexual offenders might be a consequence of multisite brain deficits which lead to disruptions in a social information-emotionality chain. This has important implications suggesting more vigilance in assessing for these deficits and developing treatment which might assist those afflicted from overcoming these deficits.

The following paper is also by the team in Vienna. In this paper, the authors show that the higher rate of minimal brain abnormalities detected through magnetic resonance imaging in a sample of highly violent incarcerated sexual offenders compared to a low violent group is also associated with self perceptions of aggression, self concepts and interpersonal problems. The implication of this study is that among offenders with minimal brain abnormalities, there are a number of psychological, social, and cultural factors linked to their violent behavior. This further indicates the need to take a biopsychosocial perceptive to understanding sexual offending.

In the next paper, the Vienna team further test their thesis that violent behavior is linked to brain abnormalities. The results of this study add to the evidence that brain abnormalities, as measured by magnetic resonance imaging, are related to violent behavior in general as well as in sex offenders. The authors suggest that in some cases of behavior disorders, it would be quite appropriate to consider including modern imaging techniques in assessment procedures. They contend that such techniques would afford a better understanding of their behavioral disorders as well as provide indications of specialized and more appropriate treatment.

The next paper turns to developments in psychological treatment. Many times, sexual offender treatment occurs in a vacuum, not involving family members directly in the process. Following the assumption that family members should be involved in the treatment of sexual offenders, Dorothy Walker presents an outcome evaluation study of a treatment program which combines the use of relapse prevention and cognitive behavior therapy techniques in concert with therapy for partners and a therapeutic nursery for preschool aged children. Because of small sample size and generally low recidivism rates, no significant results were found in her sample. However, she did find that family involvement was clearly linked to individuals staying in treatment. And, as other research results have shown, this is a key predictor of decreased recidivism. Certainly, more research is needed here, however combining a family systems approach with traditional relapse prevention and cognitive behavioral techniques should seriously be considered in many treatment programs.

While we have learned quite a bit about treating adult male sexual offenders, we know very little about other populations especially females, adolescents, or individuals with mental or physical disabilities. Dr. L. C. Miccio-Fonseca presents rare data on adolescent and adult female sex offenders in her paper. She compared female sexual offenders to male sexual offenders and other females who had not committed sexual offenses. Not surprisingly, females differed from their male counterparts and from non-offending females on a number of psychological, life-stressor, and sexual variables. The findings point to important differences between men and women offenders who commit sex crimes. These differences may indicate that female sexual offenders require more education in family planning, parenting, addressing developmental issues in childhood, safer sex methods, and birth control information. Dr. Miccio-Fonseca also found that the women were more likely to have been physically or sexually abused in their family system. Like Dorothy Walker, she calls for more treatment which includes family therapy as part of treatment. While this study reports on a small sample of female sexual offenders, it points to the importance for looking for differences and adapting treatment to address these differences. More research is obviously needed in this area.

Finally, we include an article regarding treating pedophiles who are mentally retarded and have mental and physical handicaps. Thomas Keating describes his novel approach to treating these dual or multiply diagnosed individuals. Because of cognitive deficiencies, this treatment treats this population with understanding and "respect" of their cognitive limitations. Too often, we blame the patient when they fail treatment and we don't look at the limitations of our treatment approaches. Beyond describing a novel approach to treating this very difficult population, Mr. Keating emphasizes a humanistic approach to the treatment of sexual offenders–emphasizing the concept that rehabilitation is to "reinvest with dignity." We find this to be a powerful concept and one which would be applicable to all populations. And, it embodies an essential element to good therapy–respecting the client.

Through this sampling of new research on the treatment of sexual offenders, we hope that it will stimulate therapists to refine their therapeutic approaches to the treatment of sexual offenders. We also hope to stimulate further research in the area. It is clear from the papers included in this volume that we have much more to learn.

To summarize the entire conference and the many wonderful research papers that were presented would be impossible. However, there were several themes which pointed to a future direction in research in the treatment of sexual offenders. We share the following conclusions:

1. We need more research to understand risk factors associated with the development of sex offending behavior. Such investigations much include biological, as well as psycho-social influences.
2. Clearly we are finding differences between offenders that are associated with the level of violence in their crimes. We need to understand these differences, which may have implications for the development of different treatment approaches and treatment amenability. However, this further emphasizes the point that sexual offenders are simply not a homogenous population. We will be more likely to improve treatment effectiveness when

we carefully evaluate each individual and individualize their treatment given their particular deficiencies.

3. We need more research on healthy sexual development which might shed light on the development of aberrant sexual behavior. We lack data of what is normal and only have data on developmental histories from sexual offenders or individuals with behavioral disorders.

4. We need more research on paraphilias compared to non-paraphilic compulsive sexual behavior. We need to understand the similarities and differences of these behaviors.

5. We need to understand better the process of psychotherapy. Especially when working with special populations, it is important to understand how the therapeutic process works, what are the "active ingredients" to sexual offender treatment, and how is the process and substance of sexual offender treatment influenced by ethnicity, gender, age, and developmental deficits.

6. New research is increasing in the use of various pharmacotherapies. We need more controlled studies analyzing the effectiveness of these medications.

7. There is continued debate about the effectiveness of castration. We need to take a scientific approach to considering this as a treatment option taking into consideration the serious ethical and humanitarian concerns given this extremely invasive treatment approach.

8. We need research evaluating the effects of recently enacted sexual predator laws in the United States of America (USA) allowing for indefinite civil commitment and Megan's Law (USA) requiring sex offenders to register and to notify communities when and where a sex offender is being released into the community from prison.

9. Finally, we need more studies on recidivism. Many of the previous studies were done using fairly primitive techniques and our research continues to use weak methodology. To refine our methods, we need to re-analyze how effective we can be with various populations of sexual offenders, take into account the heterogeneity of this population and to refine our evaluation research.

This is an exciting area of investigation. We hope this volume stimulates more research with more rigorous experimental designs, greater understanding of sexual offenders and, ultimately, promotes improved treatment for sexual offenders around the world.

REFERENCES

Association for the Treatment of Sexual Abusers. (1997). *Ethical Standards and Principles for the Management of Sexual Abusers*. Beaverton, Oregon: Author.

Coleman, E., Dwyer, S. M., Abel, G., Berner, W., Breiling, J., Hindman, J., Honey-Knopp, F., Langevin, R., & Pfafflin, F. (1996). Standards of care for the treatment of adult sex offenders. *Journal of Offender Rehabilitation, 22 (3/4),* 5-11.

Standards of Care for the Treatment of Adult Sex Offenders

Eli Coleman, PhD
S. Margretta Dwyer, MA
Gene Abel, MD
Wolfgang Berner, MD
James Breiling, PhD
Reinhard Eher, MD
Jan Hindman, MA
Ron Langevin, PhD
Thore Langfeldt, PhD
Michael Miner, PhD
Friedemann Pfäfflin, MD
Peter Weiss, PhD

SUMMARY. A proposed version of these standards was first produced and published in the *Journal of Offender Rehabilitation* through input from professional meetings (Coleman and Dwyer, 1990). Since that time, The Standards of Care were reviewed and revised by a group of professionals and unanimously endorsed by voice vote by the participants in the Third International Congress on the Treatment of Sex Offenders held in Minneapolis, Minnesota, September 20-22, 1994. These Standards were again published in the *Journal of Offender Rehabilitation* (Coleman, Dwyer, Abel, Berner, Breiling, Hindman, Honey-Knopp, Langevin, and Pfäfflin, 1996). Those Standards have been sub-

Address correspondence to Eli Coleman, PhD, Professor and Director, Program in Human Sexuality, School of Medicine, University of Minnesota, 1300 South 2nd Street, Suite 180, Minneapolis, MN 55454 USA (E-mail: colem001@tc.umn.edu).

[Haworth co-indexing entry note]: "Standards of Care for the Treatment of Adult Sex Offenders." Coleman et al. Co-published simultaneously in *Journal of Psychology & Human Sexuality* (The Haworth Press, Inc.) Vol. 11, No. 3, 2000, pp. 11-17; and: *Sexual Offender Treatment: Biopsychosocial Perspectives* (ed: Eli Coleman, and Michael Miner) The Haworth Press, Inc., 2000, pp. 11-17. Single or multiple copies of this article are available for a fee from The Haworth Document Delivery Service [1-800-342-9678, 9:00 a.m. - 5:00 p.m. (EST). E-mail address: getinfo@haworthpressinc.com].

© 2000 by The Haworth Press, Inc. All rights reserved.

sequently reviewed by the current authors at the Fifth International Conference on the Treatment of Sex Offenders held in Caracas, Venezuela, March 22-27, 1998 and minor modifications and changes were incorporated into this version. The authors invite feedback from readers. Further revisions are anticipated and will be reviewed by current committee members and at future International Conferences on the Treatment of Sexual Offenders. *[Article copies available for a fee from The Haworth Document Delivery Service: 1-800-342-9678. E-mail address: getinfo@haworthpressinc.com <Website: http://www.haworthpressinc.com>]*

KEYWORDS. Sexual offenders, sexual offenses, assessment, treatment

A paraphilia is a condition of compulsive response to, or dependence upon, an unusual and unacceptable stimulus in the imagery of fantasy, for optimal initiation and fantasy during solo masturbation or sexual activity with a partner. There are well over 40 types of paraphilias which have been identified and defined (Money, 1986). Only eight of them are listed in the *Diagnostic and Statistical Manual of Mental Disorders* (American Psychiatric Association, 1994), where the remainder are subsumed under, "not otherwise specified." Given the socio-cultural-religious-political climate, some paraphilias are legally considered to be sex crimes which are punishable by law. In legal codes, crimes against nature and affronts to socially acceptable sexual behavior are criminalized and are regarded as sexual offenses. These crimes have included statutory rape, violent rape, child molesting, exhibitionism, voyeurism and incest. What is considered a sexual crime and the standards of punishment are state, time, and culture dependent. Over time, there have been many revisions of the criminal sexual codes (Pallone, 1990).

For the most part, today sexual offenders may be fined, ordered to psychological or medical treatment, and/or imprisoned. For first-time offenders, and for lesser offenses, there is a greater likelihood of probation, subject to some specific professional sexual offender treatment.

Although treatment is costly and unaffordable by some, not to treat can be more costly emotionally and psychologically for the offender, for the victims and future victims, and for society. The predominant view of the lay public around the world is that sexual crimes can be eradicated with punishment, indeterminate incarceration and/or death. This predominant view is not supported by scientific evidence, and the scientific community needs to continue to promote awareness that sexual crimes can be the manifestations of biomedical/psychiatric/ psychological illnesses for which people must be treated, rather than simply punished.

In recent decades, the demand for sexual offender treatment has increased, as have the number and variety of possible biomedical/psychiatric/psychological treatments. The rationale upon which such treatments have been offered has become more and more complex. Various "appropriate care" philosophies have been suggested by many professionals who have identified themselves as experts on the topic of sexual offenders.

In an effort to establish minimal acceptable guidelines for the treatment of sexual offenders, the authors present the following Standards of Care as guidelines which might be helpful to enhance the ethical and professional treatment of sexual offenders throughout the world.

STATEMENT OF PURPOSE

Although each profession has its own standards of care, the following are minimal recommendations of Standards of Care. It is recommended that professionals involved in the treatment of sexual offenders use the following *minimal criteria* for the evaluation of their work. It is recommended that the reasons for exceptions to these standards, in the management of any individual case, be very carefully documented.

DEFINITIONS

Standards of Care

Standards of Care are exactly what is implied: standards for caring for patients. In this case: care and treatment of sexual offenders.

Paraphilia

Paraphilia is an erotosexual condition occurring in men and women who are responsive to, or dependent upon, an unusual or socially unacceptable stimulus in imagery or fantasy for initiation and maintenance of erotic-sexual arousal and the facilitation or attainment of orgasm.

Sexual Offense

A sexual offense involves engaging in illegal sexual behavior which is defined by criminal statutes. It should be also noted that there is great discrepancy throughout the world as to what constitutes a sexual offense. (Pallone, 1990)

Sexual Offender

An individual who commits a sexual crime as legally defined in his or her own culture legal jurisdiction.

Psychological Treatment

Psychological treatment refers to the array of therapies which have been designed to treat sexual offenders. Different treatments are based on different psychological and psychiatric theories regarding the origin of the paraphilic sexual offending, for example, psychoanalytic, cognitive, behavioral, social learning, and family systems theories. Psychological or psychiatric care can be provided in individual, couple, family or group settings. The purpose of treatment is to prevent further offending behavior and further victimization of others.

Biomedical Treatment

Biomedical treatment refers to the use of pharmacological treatment. Pharmacologic therapy has included (but is not limited to) the use of antiandrogens, antidepressants, and antianxiety, antiepileptic, antipsychotic, and/or other medications.

PROFESSIONAL COMPETENCE

Possession of an academic degree in behavioral science, medicine, or for the provision of psychosocial clinical services does not necessarily attest to the possession of sufficient competence to conduct assessment or treatment of paraphilic or sexual offending problems. Persons assessing and/or treating sexual offenders should have clinical training and experience in the diagnosis and treatment of a range of psychiatric and psychological conditions and also specialized training and experience in the assessment and treatment of paraphilic and sexual offender problems. This would generally be reflected by appropriate licensure as a psychiatrist, psychologist, or clinical therapist and by documentation of training and experience in the diagnosis and treatment of a broad range of sexual conditions, including paraphilic disorders and sexual offenses. Treatment providers must be competent in making a differential diagnosis.

The following *minimal standards* for a professional should be adhered to:

1. A minimum of a master's degree or it's equivalent or medical degree in a clinical field granted by an institution of education accredited by a national/regional accrediting board or institution.
2. Demonstrated competence in therapy and indicated by a license (or its equivalent from a certifying body) to practice medicine, psychology, clinical social work, professional counseling, or marriage and family counseling.
3. Demonstrated specialized competence in counseling and diagnosis of sexual disorders and sexual offending behaviors as documentable by training or supervised clinical experience, along with continuing education.
4. Demonstrated training and competence in providing psychotherapy.

ANTECEDENTS TO SEXUAL OFFENDER TREATMENT

1. Prospective patients should receive an extensive evaluation of their sexual offending behavior and their overall sexual health. It would also include appropriateness for treatment, amenability for treatment, psychological/psychiatric diagnoses, and evaluation for the safety and protection for the community.
2. A thorough physical examination is recommended especially when physical problems are suspected that might require specific treatment, i.e., heart problems, high blood pressure, liver damage, brain lesions, and epilepsy.
3. Prospective patients should receive a psychological and/or psychiatric examination which would rule out other psychological/

psychiatric disorders. If any other psychological/psychiatric disorders are found, treatment of such disorder requires treatment in addition to their treatment for their paraphiliac or sexual offending behavior.

4. If medication is deemed necessary or requested by the patient, the patient must be given information regarding the benefits and potential side effects or disadvantages of biomedical treatment.

THE PRINCIPLES OF THE STANDARDS OF CARE

Principle 1: There is evidence that some kinds of treatment may be effective in managing and reducing recidivism with some types of sexual offenders.

Principle 2: Sexual offender treatment is viewed by offenders as an elective process (the choice is theirs), since individuals may not view their sexual offending behavior as psychologically or medically pathological.

Principle 3: The evaluation of treatment of sexual offenders requires specialized skills not usually associated with the professional training of clinical therapists or medical professionals.

Principle 4: Sexual offender treatment is performed for the purpose of improving quality of life and is considered a humane treatment for people who have committed a sexual offense and to prevent the patient from engaging in further sexual offending behavior.

Principle 5: The patient with a documented biomedical abnormality is first treated by procedures commonly accepted as appropriate for any such medical conditions before beginning, or in conjunction with, psychotherapy.

Principle 6: The patient having a psychiatric diagnosis (i.e., schizophrenia) is first treated by procedures commonly accepted as appropriate for the psychiatric diagnoses, or if appropriate, for both.

Principle 7: Sexual offender treatment may involve a variety of therapeutic approaches. It is important for professionals to keep abreast of this growing and developing field and provide the most efficacious treatments which have been demonstrated through outcome studies.

Principle 8: A treatment plan may involve the use of pharmacotherapy which may relieve some sexual arousal and fantasy and some individuals may feel less driven.

Principle 9: Professionals who work with sexual offenders should be prepared to work with the criminal justice system in a professional and cooperative manner.

Principle 10: Sexual offenders often have a need for follow-up treatment/visits, and this should be encouraged or possibly required.

Principle 11: It is unethical to charge patients for services which are essentially for research or which do not directly benefit the patient.

Principle 12: In order to effectively persuade the professionals in the legal community as well as society in general about the efficacy of sexual offender treatment, professionals should cooperate with and carry out scientifically sound treatment outcome research.

Principle 13: Sexual offenders often must face legal proceedings, and professionals treating these individuals must be prepared to appear in court if necessary.

Principle 14: Sexual offenders are given the same rights to medical and psychological privacies as any other patient group, with the exception of where the law requires otherwise, i.e., reporting laws, subpoenaing of records.

Principle 15: Sexual offenders should not be discriminated against based on age, gender, race, ethnicity, national origin, religious beliefs, socio-economic status, or physical or mental disability.

Principle 16: Professionals who treat sexual offenders must view these individuals with dignity and respect. If they fail to view the offender or their offense with compassion, then the professional should make a proper referral.

REFERENCES

American Psychiatric Association. (1994). *Diagnostic and Statistical Manual of the American Psychiatric Association (DSM-IV)*. Washington, DC: The American Psychiatric Association.

Coleman, E. And Dwyer, S.M. (1990). Proposed standards of care for the treatment of adult sex offenders. *Journal of Offender Rehabilitation, 16 (1/2)*, 93-106.

Coleman, E., Dwyer, S.M., Abel, G., Berner, W., Breiling, J., Hindman, J., Honey-Knopp, F., Langevin, R., & Phafflin, F. (1996). Standards of care for the treatment of adult sex offenders. *Journal of Offender Rehabilitation, 22 (3/4)*, 5-11.

Money, J. (1986). *Lovemaps: Clinical Concepts of Sexual/Erotic Health & Pathology, Paraphilia, and Gender Transposition in Childhood, Adolescence & Maturity*. Buffalo: Prometheus.

Pallone, N.J. (1990). *Rehabilitating Criminal Sexual Psychopaths: Legislative Mandates. Clinical Quandaries*. New Brunswick, NJ: Transaction Books.

The Psychoneuroendocrinology
of (Sexual) Aggression

Ritsaert Lieverse, MD
Louis J. G. Gooren, MD
Johanna Assies, MD

SUMMARY. The contours of the psychoneuroendocrinology of (sexual) aggression are becoming clearer. The sex difference in aggression originally directed attention to androgens, but the role of androgens has been difficult to substantiate. Rather novel is the insight that (sexual) aggression may be viewed as a maladaptive stress response. The stress response system is composed of psychological elements (the interpretation and labeling of threats), the neural system, that subserves this interpretation, and finally the endocrine system permitting the organism to react to threats with a physical response such as flight or fight, and as such is vital for our self-protection. Aggression may be viewed as an inappropriate and exaggerated response to a perceived threat. The stress system is largely tuned by early life experiences. Both psychological and biological elements can be identified in the stress response system, allowing both psychotherapeutic and pharmacological approaches to treatment. *[Article copies available for a fee from The Haworth Document Delivery Service: 1-800-342-9678. E-mail address: getinfo@haworthpressinc.com <Website: http://www.haworthpressinc.com>]*

Ritsaert Lieverse and Johanna Assies are affiliated with the Departments of Endocrinology and Psychiatry, Academic Medical Center, Amsterdam, the Netherlands. Louis J. G. Gooren is affiliated with the Department of Endocrinology of the hospital of the Vrije Universiteit.

Address correspondence to Louis Gooren, MD, Endo/AZVU, P. O. Box 7057, 1007 MB Amsterdam, the Netherlands (E-mail: lgooren@inter.nl.net).

[Haworth co-indexing entry note]: "The Psychoneuroendocrinology of (Sexual) Aggression." Lieverse, Ritsaert, Louis J. G. Gooren, and Johanna Assies. Co-published simultaneously in *Journal of Psychology & Human Sexuality* (The Haworth Press, Inc.) Vol. 11, No. 3, 2000, pp. 19-36; and: *Sexual Offender Treatment: Biopsychosocial Perspectives* (ed: Eli Coleman, and Michael Miner) The Haworth Press, Inc., 2000, pp. 19-36. Single or multiple copies of this article are available for a fee from The Haworth Document Delivery Service [1-800-342-9678, 9:00 a.m. - 5:00 p.m. (EST). E-mail address: getinfo@haworthpressinc.com].

© 2000 by The Haworth Press, Inc. All rights reserved.

19

KEYWORDS. Sexual aggression, violence, brain, testosterone, adrenal

Aggression in general, and this applies also to sexual aggression, is not a unitary phenomenon. Aggression maybe motivated by a large variety of reasons. Aggression has long been and still is viewed as a moral or ethical question and has been largely the domain of the humanistic sciences exploring its psychological and/or environmental roots.

Only in the past 25 years there has been an interest in the biology of (sexual) aggression. This has been a cumbersome exploration since there are so many intervening variables blurring the view on the biological underpinnings of human aggression, such as early life experiences, personality disorders and environment to name a few (Barratt & Slaughter, 1998). Aggression is not an all-or-none phenomenon. All human beings experience angers and may display aggression given enough provocation. The biological sciences, as every branch of scientific endeavor, are reductionistic and attempt to limit intervening variables to the smallest number possible in order to bring to light biological components of a complicated phenomenon such as aggression. Methodologically, reductionism is inescapable to uncover the biology of (sexual) aggression. Once we have arrived at an understanding, it must be integrated again with other relevant factors of a psychological or social nature. In the biomedical sciences it is then common practice to resort to animal experimentation in the hope that these can provide acceptably unbiased information how things operate from a biological viewpoint. Animal experimentation allows, to a much larger extent, to control the number of variables than is the case in the human. Of most laboratory animals the life span is relatively short so that certain (early) life experiences can be taken into account when their adult life behavior is studied, which is an advantage.

In animals several categories of aggressive behavior can be identified such as offensive, defensive, predatory, fear-induced, territorial, irritable, sex-related and maternal aggression (Albert, Walch & Jonik, 1993). It is an unresolved question whether all these categories have distinct neurological and hormonal systems underlying their biological execution and what the counterparts are in the human. This question is of interest since a thorough understanding would allow to identify biological predispositions to (sexual) aggression and violence. A better understanding of the neurobiology of (sexual) aggression in terms of neurotransmitters and hormones would allow the development of pharmacological treatment modalities. Together with other treatment strategies (psychological treatment, social rehabilitation), this could help individuals to control their aggressive impulses and to help them to lead more meaningful lives with respect of the rights of their fellow human beings.

This contribution will address three areas of biological research, which have links with the biology of (sexual aggression):

1. Androgen-related (sexual) aggression. The role and importance of androgens is often misconceptualized, This contribution will argue that androgens as such show no consistent relation with aggression. Its main function is to lower the threshold for sexual events to occur. If sexual events are of an aggressive nature in an individual's life, they may become better amenable with pharmacological intervention reducing the biological effects of androgens.

2. Aggression may be related to anatomical or functional disorders of certain brain areas.

3. Aggression as a stress response disorder. A fascinating area of research is the psychoneuroendocrine substrate of stress. There have been major advances over the last decades. The biological systems of human beings and animals alike, are not closed systems; there is an interaction with the environment. Every internal and external stimulus is interpreted and assessed. Life exists by maintaining a complex dynamic equilibrium, or homeostasis, that is constantly challenged by extrinsic and intrinsic adverse forces (Stratakis & Chrousos, 1994). The organism reacts to this threatened homeostasis with the activation of a complex of behavioral responses evoking fright, flight or fight as defense mechanisms, to preserve integrity. This contribution argues that aggression and violence are maladaptive response mechanisms in reaction to intrinsic and extrinsic stimuli of a system that in essence is designed to confer protection to an organism.

ANDROGEN RELATED AGGRESSION

For over 30 years there have been attempts to relate testosterone to aggression in humans. It is not unreasonable to assume that these attempts have been inspired by the much higher prevalence of violence and sexual aggression in adult men as compared to women. The much higher testosterone blood levels in adult men than in women seem to provide an obvious explanation, and inferences have been made that aggressive women have higher testosterone levels than controls. But laboratory studies of human aggression have shown that at least under laboratory conditions adult men and women have similar propensities towards aggression (Eagly & Steffen, 1986). Also domestic violence and homicide within marriage are not strongly sex different (see United States Department of Justice, 1977, 1980-1990). It might be that factors not immediately related to the psychotropic effects of testosterone play a role in the male dominance in violence and (sexual) aggression. Men are on average physically larger and stronger. These physical properties and the mood-elevating effects of testosterone may increase assertiveness, and if uncontrolled, the threshold for aggression may become low. Men receive a different socialization with a likely greater acceptance of using force. Men incur also more brain accidents causing brain damage which sometimes reduce inhibitions to use force and engage in violence (Cobb, Cairns, Miles and Cairns, 1995).

The study of high-and low-aggression groups has not produced consistent support for the argument that blood or salivary testosterone levels are consistently and significantly related to violence or (sexual) aggression in either men or women. Studies show deficiencies in design and measurements of testosterone (for review see Albert, Walsh & Jonik, 1993).

From a (clinical) endocrinological viewpoint there are no convincing arguments that testosterone, as such, stimulates violence. On the contrary, in conditions with strong elevations of testosterone levels there is convincing evidence that such an effect does not occur. Puberty in boys is associated with a strong increase in testosterone which is not correlated to aggression (Sussman, Inoff-Germain, Lairiaux, Cutler & Chrousos, 1987). There may be an increase in assertiveness but aggression is not the normal consequence of puberty.

Male contraceptive studies have used testosterone regimens, which elevate circulating testosterone levels to 100-150% above normal. An undue increase in (sexual) aggression was only rarely noted (in 1-2% of men in the study) (Bagatell, Heiman, Matsumoto, Rivier & Bremner, 1994). Certain pathological conditions in women, such as polycystic ovaries or adrenal disease, are associated with elevated blood testosterone levels, which are much higher than encountered in aggressive female prison inmates. Nevertheless women with these medical conditions are not more aggressive than controls (see Albert, Walsh & Jonik, 1993).

So called 'roid rage' has been found as an effect of the use of high doses of anabolic androgenic steroids. Several case reports and also larger studies have found adverse effects on aggression, but this is not universal (see Bahrke, Yesalis & Wright, 1990). In view of the millions of users worldwide these manifestations are relatively rare and may be related to an inherently more psychopathological and aggressive personality of the users (see Yates, Perry & Murry, 1992) rather than the actions of androgens per se.

Some studies of sex offenders have found that medication reducing the biological action of testosterone resulted also in a reduction in aggression though to a variable degree (Bradford, 1983). This may be due to the devitalizing and mood depressing effects that such drug interventions sometimes imply rather than to a pharmacological effect on aggressivity as such (Dixson, 1980; Francis, 1981).

However, below some evidence will be provided that indirectly testosterone may be linked to a greater vulnerability of men to display aggressive behavior. In an indirect way testosterone may predispose men to maladaptive stress responses.

In summary, it has been impossible to relate testosterone consistently and systematically to (sexual) aggression. Testosterone has a clear effect on sexual desire and arousability (see Gijs & Gooren, 1996). Pharmacological interventions reducing the biological actions of testosterone can be expected to be helpful in those types of paraphilias characterized by intense and frequent *sexual* desire and sexual arousal. Some of these paraphilias may include aggression and violence and then qualify for anti-androgenic interventions (Gijs & Gooren, 1996).

ANATOMICAL AND FUNCTIONAL DISORDERS
OF THE BRAIN

In humans there are two well documented cases reporting aggressive behavior related to tumors in the medial hypothalamus and a number where this relation is less well established (see Alpers, 1937; Reeves & Plum, 1969). The assumption that the tumors are causally related to aggressive behavior comes from experiments in rats where lesions of the hypothalamus increase (defensive) aggressive behavior. This aggression is manifest in both intact and gonadectomized (testosterone-deprived) animals (Albert, Dyson & Walch, 1987; Albert, Petrovic & Walch, 1989; Albert, Walch, Zalys & Dyson, 1986).

Tumors in the septal area in humans are also associated with an increase of defensive aggressiveness (Zeman & King, 1958). The lesson to be learned is that when persons without a history of violence display unreasonable aggressive behavior, the possibility of a tumor in these brain areas must be considered.

Aggressivity may be associated with seizure activity in the temporal lobe and maybe even specifically in the amygdala (Devinsky & Bear, 1984; Fenwick, 1991; Sano, Mayanagi, Sekino, Ogashiwa & Isjima, 1970). Two types of drugs have been shown to be beneficial: Propranolol (Sheard, 1984) and the anticonvulsant Carbamazepine (Sheard, 1984; Mattes, 1990).

(SEXUAL) AGGRESSION
AS A MALADAPTIVE STRESS RESPONSE

Living organisms are constantly balancing intrinsic and extrinsic disturbing forces to maintain and protect their integrity and subjective well-being. The forces to maintain this equilibrium are a complex of physiological and behavioral adaptive responses. Those responses occur at the level of the central nervous system, which prepares systems peripherally in the body to interpret and to act on this arousal. Subsequently, in the central nervous system pathways mediating arousal, vigilance, attention, readiness to fight or flight are activated. As a result, in the peripheral body systems adaptive processes for self-protection are put into action to promote a redirection of energy in preparation for flight or fight, whatever is deemed as most appropriate protection. The central and peripheral alert systems are closely interlinked.

The psychoneuroendocrinology of this homeostasis is increasingly understood and it offers an attractive theoretical model for understanding aggression and violence (De Kloet, Korte, Rots & Kruk, 1996; Koolhaas, Meerlo, De Boer, Strubbe & Bohus, 1997). Aggressive violence can be viewed as maladaptive response mechanisms in reaction to intrinsic and extrinsic stimuli. Aggression and violence may be overreactions to a perceived threat, far in excess of what would be appropriate. This basically biological model recognizes (early) life development as an important modifier of the stress response; it influences the timing and strength of counteracting forces to perceived stress, thus impairing checks and balances of aggression. Infancy, childhood and adolescence associated with increased biological dependency and physiological and psychological immaturity may all entail increased vulnerability to develop maladaptive stress responses (Bowlby, 1969; Bowlby, 1984; Cicchetti, 1984; Field & Reite, 1985). What constitutes no threat to one individual may evoke a violent response in another subject. Activation of the stress system occurs in diametrically opposed situations, such as pleasure and dysphoria. Self-driven activation of the stress system is associated with pleasure if adaptive, controlled and proportionate, and dysphoria if maladaptive, uncontrolled and disproportionate (Stratakis & Chrousos, 1994).

The Neuroendocrinology of the Stress-System

One component is the locus coeruieus-norepinephrine system in the brain stem, which when activated, releases norepinephrine from a dense network of neurons in the brain leading to arousal. The peripheral effectors are the sympathetic nerves and the adrenal medulla. The other component is the corticotropin-releasing hormone (CRH). The CRH system is widespread in the central nervous system but the highest concentration of CRH is found in the paraventricular nucleus of the hypothalamus.

CRH is the principal stimulus for the pituitary to secrete adrenocorticotropic hormone (ACTH), which in turn stimulates the adrenocortex to produce cortisol. The understanding of the hypothalamus-pituitary-adrenal axis and the availability of synthetic CRH and ACTH and adrenal hormones have allowed to test this system in a large number of psychological and psychiatric conditions. The responses obtained have provided a better understanding of the biology of stress and adaptation. The 'tuning' of the hypothalamus-pituitary-adrenal axis is a sort of window into the brain, offering insight into the state of activity of the biology of certain mental processes.

Endocrine systems are characterized by feedback mechanisms ensuring a degree of control over the activity of the system. Adrenal hormones feedback on the components of the hypothalamus-pituitary-adrenal axis and its connections in the brain providing counter regulations and thus avoiding over responses in the activation of the alarm system. Deficient feedback inhibition may lead to overreactivity of the system, leading to inappropriate responses to perceived threat.

The Limbic System

For the sake of simplicity the two components of the stress system were presented as isolated mechanisms but in reality they are not. First of all these two systems interact so that activation of one implies activation of the other. But stress is a matter of personal interpretation and assessment and the stress system depicted above is a kind of common pathway of arousal in response to intrinsic and extrinsic stimuli and their context (Van der Kolk & Saporta, 1993).

So, the stress mechanisms are an integral part of a number of elements of the brain related to the retrievability and to logical, and even more important, emotional analysis of the information: the initiation of action on the basis of this analysis is modulated by the emotional tone (Rainey, Aleem, Oritz, Yaragani, Pohl & Berchow, 1987; Squire, 1987).

The sensitivity and responsiveness of the integrated systems are directed by genetic factors and by environmental factors in early development and by the present state of psychological functioning.

The attraction of these recent discoveries lies in the fact that this biological system clearly leave room for, so to say, non-biological factors such as (early) life experiences, and for the benefits that therapy of a biological nature may offer. Psychotherapy offers opportunities for a subject to arrive at different labelings and interpretations of intrinsic and extrinsic (threatening) stimuli, to learn to recognize certain habitual responses and take appropriate measures; this will be translated into a different, ideally a more cohesive, more controlled pattern of arousal. Another advantage of this theoretical model is that it lets us understand that psychotropic medication may be of use and how they may be an integral part of a package of therapeutical strategies.

Early Brain Development and Early Stress

Humans share this stress response mechanism with a large number of animals, among them laboratory animals which have allowed extensive experimentation. Stressful experience during early brain development appears to produce profound biologically demonstrable alterations in several mechanism of adaptation (Lewis, 1992).

Several signs of behavioral and neuroendocrine disfunctioning can be related to exposure to neonatal stress and is evidenced in the functional state, the 'tuning' of the hypothalamus-pituitary-adrenal axis (Konner, 1982; Tennes, 1982). The biological mechanism of this 'imprinting of a deprived infancy on the brain' is probably the encoding of receptors of CRH and adrenal hormones in brain areas that are relevant for arousal and for the regulation of the hypothalamus-pituitary-adrenal axis. Stress hormones exert their action on the brain through these receptors. The number of receptors and other properties may modulate the effects of stress hormones on the brain, which is 'organized' early in life. The effects of the early environment on the 'tuning' of the response characteristics of the hypothalamus-pituitary-adrenal axis are an expression of the plasticity of the brain in early development. Factors such as maternal care are able to program, to organize rudimentary biological responses to threatening stimuli preparing the developing organism to act to the demands of the environment (Field & Reite, 1985; Konner, 1982; Tennes, 1982). Such responses then become habitual and are relatively (but not totally) resistant to change.

The hippocampus records the spatial and temporal dimensions of experiences in memory; it does not fully mature until the third and fourth year of life. However the system that subserves memory related to the quality (feel and sounds) of things (located in the amygdala) matures much earlier. Thus in the first few years of life, only the quality of events but not their context can be remembered. Severe or prolonged stress suppresses hippocampal functioning (Squire 1987), creating context free fearful associations which are, in retrospect, hard to locate in space and time. These may result in amnesia for experiences which were originally associated with the severe stress (see also Van der Kolk & Saporta, 1993). This may explain rage-outbursts, without much reason or context and which are therefore difficult to interpret which can be observed in murderers, in aggressors and moreover victims of sexual rape.

Neurotransmitters

In the above neuroendocrine system neurons communicate electrophysiologically with each other by means of neurotransmitters. These are chemical substances secreted by one neuron and taken up by receptors of adjacent neurons. As in all biological systems this is a matter of checks and balances; neurotransmitters feedback on their secreting neurons. Interference with this electrochemical process of neurotransmission (addition or inhibition) provides an opportunity to tune the biological substrate of our mental functioning. A number of neurotransmitters have been implicated in the biochemical basis of aggressive behavior in the human.

First the catecholamines; there is a correlation between aggressiveness and high blood and urinary norepinephrine levels (for review see: Haller, Makara & Kruk, 1998). In the cerebrospinal fluid (in close contact with the central nervous system) high levels of the metabolites of norepinephrine can be found in aggression (Coccaro, 1996; Haller, Makara & Kruk, 1998).

Secondly dopamine; a decreased central dopamine secretary tonus has been suggested as a parallel of aggressiveness and administration of dopaminergic drugs have been followed by a reduction of aggressive behavior in psychotic patients (Gerra, Avazini, Zainovic, Fertonani, Caccavari, Delsignore, Gardini, Talarico, Lecchini, Maestri & Bambilla, 1996). A telltale of central dopamine tonus is the peripheral blood level of the pituitary hormone prolactin and indeed low blood levels of prolactin correlate with hostility and anger (Gerra, Avazini, Zainovic, Fertonani, Caccavari, Delsignore, Gardini, Talarico, Lecchini, Maestri & Rambilla, 1996).

Thirdly serotonin; (Virkkunen, Goldman, Nielsen & Linnoila, 1995). Several recent reviews have concluded that reduced serotonin activity in the central nervous system is one of the biological correlates of impaired impulse control. This hypothesized relation has been corroborated in animal experimentation. Studies in humans (Asberg, 1997; Linnoila, 1996) show a consistent pattern: men who engage in impulsive, unplanned acts of interpersonal violence have lower levels of 5-hydroxyindoleacetic acid (5-HIAA), the major metabolite of serotonin in the cerebrospinal fluid (Asberg, 1997; Linnoila, 1996). In both humans and nonhuman primates, 5-HIAA levels in the cerebrospinal fluid show a traitlike stability across time (Highley, Mehlman, Oland, Taub, Vickers, Suomi & Linnoila, 1996). There is now evidence that genetic factors play a role in the low turnover of serotonin in the brain. Enzymes affect the biochemistry of serotonin synthesis. Gene expression regulates enzyme activity, which in turn determines activity of neurotransmitter systems (Nielsen, Goldman, Virkkunen, Tokola, Rawlings & Linnoila, 1994).

Brain serotonin and dopamine metabolisms mutually regulate each other (Asberg, 1997; Coccaro, 1996; De Kloet, 1996). High free testosterone concentration in the cerebrospinal fluid is associated with competitive aggression and this may be functional and positive in combination with a normal serotonergic tonus. But a decreased serotonergic tonus in combination with testosterone may produce disregulated aggression of physically damaging proportions (Highley, Mehlman, Oland, Taub, Vickers, Suomi & Linnoila, 1996). This information may help us to understand why in some cases testosterone is a factor in (sexual) violence, namely when normal levels of testosterone coincide with a low serotonin activity in the brain.

Sex-Differences in Stress-Disorders

Gonadal sex-steroids may affect hypothalamic-pituitary-adrenal axis of the stress system and the differences in sex steroid concentration between men and women may be a factor in understanding sex-differences in aggression and violence. CRH and arginine-vasopressin stimulate the secretion of ACTH. Sex steroids influence their synthesis. Sex steroids also influence the binding properties of corticosteroid receptors in the brain centers related to activation of the LHPA-axis, thus affecting the tuning of one of the stress systems (see McEwen, 1987). In rat experiments it has been shown that sex steroids during perinatal life 'organize' the dynamics of the LHPA-axis leading to sex-differentiated patterns of activity of the LHPA-axis, that is to say it is more arousable in males than in females (Almeida, Canoine, Holsboer & Patchev, 1997). Also later in life, after puberty when sex steroids rise to adult levels, androgens as opposed to estrogens increase the arousability of the LHPA-axis (Heuser, Gotthardt, Schweiger, Schmider, Lammers, Dettling & Holsboer, 1994).

These data together show that the male has a more vulnerable stress-system. And indirectly, androgens may be a factor in misdirected stress responses occurring more frequently in the male.

The Stress-Response Disorders

The stress response system is essentially a protective mechanism for the organism, but it may become misfitting. Many psychiatric disorders are, in fact, stress-response disorders (Chrousos & Gold, 1992). Depression often is a result of chronic stress, or of stressors having occurred in early life. In the posttraumatic stress-disorder (PTSD) a traumatic stressor has misdirected the stress-response of the victim at the time of the trauma so that subsequently every future stressor is interpreted as a recurrence of that trauma (Van der Kolk & Saporta, 1993).

The posttraumatic stress disorder is in many ways related to aggression; they frequently even are inseparable (American Psychiatric Association, 1994). Aggression may be viewed as a hyperarousal symptom, as a maladaptive coping mechanism with arousal (Scarpa & Raine, 1997). It is often part of the PTSD (Carmen, Reiker & Mills, 1984). It is known that sexual trauma is much more common than formerly thought, and from the above it may become clear that an own (sexual) trauma may become an important determinant of later (sexual) aggression (Byrne & Riggs, 1996; Else, Wonderlich, Beatty, Christie & Staton, 1993). Another parallel is present in the victims of (sexual) aggression who are traumatized and often identify with the aggressor (Stockholm syndrome) or even try to gain control over their victim role by becoming an aggressor themselves, not being able to resort to more appropriate strategies to cope.

Both PTSD and aggression are maladapted reactions to stress. There are further parallels. In aggression as well as in trauma a stress-induced analgesia can be present (Van der Kolk, Greenberg, Boyd & Krystal, 1985; Irwin, 1998; Kaplan, Erensaft, Sanderson, Wetzler, Foote & Asnis, 1998). In the psychobiology this dissociative state is thought to be mediated by endogenous opioid release during stress, which function it is to kill the pain and which may be functional in an acute state of threat enabling the organism to react defensively (Irwin, 1998; Kaplan, Erensaft, Sanderson, Wetzler, Foote & Asnis, 1998). This also in part explains the rigid behavioral patterns, which impress as addictive (Byrne & Riggs, 1996). Frequently, abused children are engaged in self-destructive acts as headbanging, biting, burning and cutting (Green, 1978). Sometimes this is called an addiction to trauma, which could be the driving force behind the re-experience (Van der Kolk, Greenberg, Boyd & Krystal, 1985). In both disorders often amnesia numbs the patient's mind.

In both PTSD and in aggression a depletion of serotonin is found. In both disorders testosterone levels are in the higher ranges of what is normal (see also Mason, Giller, Kosten & Wahby, 1990). Suicidal tendencies–which can be viewed as inward-directed aggression early life are significantly correlated with depletion of serotonin system, especially in suicidal tendencies in patients with a history of trauma! (Coccaro, Kavoussi & Lesser, 1992).

Studying stress disorders, especially the PTSD, is therefore important for understanding the traumatized as well as the aggressors. Both are expressions of stress disorders. The neurobiology of the stress disorders helps us to better understand and treat aggressive patients.

PHARMACOLOGICAL INTERVENTIONS

Several classes of antidepressant drugs have been successfully used in the treatment of dysfunctional sexual behavior (Gijs & Gooren, 1996). The action of antidepressants (e.g., the tricyclic antidepressants, selective serotonin reuptake inhibitors and selective and reversible mono-amino-oxidase inhibitors) is all to increase the concentrations of the neurotransmitters norepinephrine, serotonin and to a lesser extent dopamine in the synapses between neurons. Thus a different tuning of the biological system subserving psychological function is established. The increase in concentrations of serotonin and dopamine, which were found to be low in aggressive states, may have a beneficial effect (Fava, 1997). Another mechanism of actions has been proposed. Antidepressants might restore the normal interactions between the components of the hypothalamic-pituitary-adrenal axis and reduce its hyperactivity by increasing the negative feedback action of cortisol on this system. Cortisol is one of the two peripheral limbs of the arousal and stress system of the organism (Michelson & Gold, 1994). The result is that the alarming effects of cortisol are tuned down. Selective serotonin reuptake inhibitors have been shown to be effective in normalizing the drive of the HPA-axis.

Pharmacological efforts to redress the higher arousability of the LHPA-axis in men are probably more successful when they aim at the LHPA-axis itself, instead of aiming at the less selective and indirect serotonergic cascade. In the future drugs interfering with the actions of CRH and glucocorticoids in the LHPA-axis are likely to play a role, too. Their effects are more direct in calming down the alert system.

CONCLUSIONS

The contours of the psychoneuroendocrinolgy of (sexual) aggression are becoming clearer. The obvious sex difference in aggressive responses originally directed attention to androgens as an important factor. But upon critical examination a direct role of androgens is difficult to substantiate, but its role may be indirect. Increasingly aggression is conceived of as an expression of a maladaptive stress response. The stress response system as such is vital for our self-protection allowing us to react to extrinsic and intrinsic threats with fight or flight responses. There is growing insight that (sexual) aggression may be viewed as an overreaction and therefore maladaptive stress responses. The biological underpinnings of the psychoneuroendocrinology of the stress response system are increasingly understood. And as the term psychoneuroendocrinology suggests, it is composed of psychological elements (the interpretation and labeling of threats), the neural system that subserves this interpretation, and finally there is a connection with the endocrine system which permits the organism to react to threats with physical responses such as flight or fight. It has become clear that the tuning of this stress response system is strongly influenced by early life experiences. A deprived childhood 'imprints itself on the brain' leading to an incapacity to absorb and cope with stressors and leading to unmeaning, and sometimes violent responses as self-defence in reaction to perceived threats. This theoretical model of aggression offers entries for a number of disciplines to make a contribution to the healing process of perpetrators. Both psychotherapy (learning to arrive at different interpretations) and pharmacotherapy (affecting the tuning of the stress response system) may help to restore the ill-balanced stress response system

BIBLIOGRAPHY

Albert D.J., Walch M.L. and Jonik, R. H. (1993). Aggression in humans: What is its biological foundation? *Neuroscience and Biobehavioral Reviews,* 17, 405-425.

Albert, D.J., Dyson, E.M., Walsh, M.L. (1987). Competitive behavior in male rats: Aggression and success enhanced by medial hypothalamic lesions as well as by testosterone implants. *Physiology and Behavior,* 40, 695-701.

Albert, D.J., Petrovic, D.M., Walsh, M.L. (1989). Female rats in a competitive situation: Medical hypothalamic lesions increase and ovariectomy decreases success and aggression. *Physiology and Behavior,* 46, 379-386.

Albert, D.J., Walsh, M.L., Zalys, C., Dyson, E.M. (1986). Defensive aggression towards an experimenter: No differences between males and females following septal, medial accumbens, or medial hypothalamic lesions in rats. *Physiology and Behavior,* 38, 11-14.

Almeida O.F.X., Canoine, V., Ali, S., Holsboer, F. and Patchev, V.K. (1997). Activational effects of gonadal steroids on hypothalamo-pituitary-adrenal regulation in the rat disclosed by response to dexamethasone suppression. *Journal of Neuroendocrinology,* 9, 129-134.

Alpers, B.J. (1937). Relation to the hypothalamus to disorders of personality. *Archives of Neurology and Psychiatry,* 38, 291-303.

American Psychiatric Association. (1994). *Diagnostic and Statistical Manual of mental disorders, Fourth edition.* Washington, DC.

Asberg, M. (1997). Neurotransmitters and suicidal behavior. The evidence from cerebrospinal fluid studies. *Annals of the New York Academy of Sciences,* 836, 158-181.

Bagatell, C.J., Heiman, J.R., Matsumoto, A.M., Rivier, J.E. and Bremner, W.J. (1994). Metabolic and behavioral effects of high dose exogenous testosterone in healthy men. *Journal of Clinical Endocrinology & Metabolism,* 79, 561-567.

Bahrke, M.S., Yesalis, C.E. and Wright, J.E. (1990). Psychological and behavioral effects of endogenous testosterone levels and anabolic-androgenic steroids among males. A review. *Sports Medicine,* 10, 303-337.

Barratt, E.S. and Slaughter, L. (1998). Defining, measuring, and predicting impulsive aggression: A heuristic model. *Behavioral Sciences and the Law,* 16, 285-302.

Bowlby, J. (1969). Attachment and Loss. In: *Volume I, Attachment,* Basic Books, New York.

Bowlby, J. (1984). Violence in the family as a disorder of the attachment and caregiving systems. *American Journal of Psychoanalysis,* 44, 9-27.

Bradford, J.M. (1983). The hormonal treatment of sexual offenders. *Bulletin of the American Academy of Psychiatry and Law,* 11, 159-169.

Byrne, C.A. and Riggs, D.S. (1996). The cycle of trauma; relationship aggression in male Vietnam veterans with symptoms of posttraumatic stress disorder. *Violence and Victims,* 3, 213-25.

Carmen, E.H., Reiker, P.P., and Mills, T. (1984). Victims of violence and psychiatric illness. *American Journal of Psychiatry,* 141, 378-379.

Chrousos, G.P. and Gold, P.W. (1992). The concepts of stress system disorders: Overview of behavioral and physical homeostasis. *Journal of the American Medical Association,* 267: 1244-1252.

Cicchetti, D. (1984).The emergence of developmental psychopathology. *Child Development,* 55, 1-7.

Cobb, B.K., Cairns, B. D., Miles, M.S. and Cairns, R.B. (1995). A longitudinal study of the role of sociodemographic factors and childhood aggression on adolescent injury and "close calls." *Journal of Adolescent Health,* 17 (6), 381-388.

Coccaro, E.F., Kavoussi, R.J. and Lesser, J.C. (1992). Self-and other-directed human aggression: The role of the central serotonergic system. *International Clinical Psychopharmacology,* 6 (suppl.6), 70-83.

Coccaro, E.F.(1996). Neurotransmitter correlates of impulsive aggression in humans. *Annals of the New York Academy of Sciences,* 794, 82-89.

De Kloet, E.R., Korte, S.M., Rots, N.Y., and Kruk, M.R. (1996). Stress hormones, genotype, and brain organization. Implications for aggression. *Annals of the New York Academy of Sciences.* 794: 179-91.

Devinsky, O. and Bear, D. (1975). Varieties of aggressive behavior in temporal lobe epilepsy. *American Journal of Psychiatry,* 141, 651-656.

Dixson, A.F. (1980). Androgens and aggressive behavior in primates: A review. *Aggression and Behavior,* 6, 37-67.

Eagly, A.H. and Steffen, V.J. (1986). Gender and aggressive behavior: A meta-analytic review of the social psychological literature. *Psychological Bulletin,* 100, 309-330.

Else, L.T., Wonderlich, S.A., Beatty, W.W., Christy, D.W. and Staton, R.D. (1993). Personality characteristics of men who physically abuse women. Hospital and Community Psychiatry, 44, 54-58.

Fava, M.(1997). Psychopharmacologic treatment of pathologic aggression. *Psychiatric Clinics of North America,* 20, 427-451.

Fenwick, P. (1989). The nature and management of aggression in epilepsy. *Journal of Neuropsychiatry,* 1, 418-425.

Field, T. and Reite, M., (eds.). (1985). *The psychobiology of attachment and separation.* Academic Press, Orlando.

Francis, K.T. (1981). The relationship between high and low trait psychological stress, serum testosterone, and serum cortisol. *Experentia,* 337, 1269-1297.

Gerra, G., Avazini, P., Zainovic, A., Fertonani, G., Caccavari, R., Delsignore, R., Gardini, F., Talarico, E., Lecchini, R., Maestri, D. and Brambilla, F. (1996). Neurotransmitter and endocrine modulation of aggressive behavior and its components in normal humans. *Behavioral Brain Research,* 81, 19-24.

Gijs, L. and Gooren, L. (1996). Hormonal and psychopharmacological interventions in the treatment of paraphilias: An update. *The Journal of Sex Research,* 33 (4), 273-290.

Green, A.H. (1978). Self-destructive behavior in battered children. *American Journal of Psychiatry,* 135, 579-582.

Haller, J., Makara, G.B., and Kruk, M.R. (1998). Catecholaminergic involvement in the control of aggression: Hormones, the peripheral sympathetic, and central *noradrenergic systems. Neuroscience and Biobehavioral Reviews,* 22, 85-97.

Heuser, I.J., Gotthardt, U., Schweiger, U., Schmider, J., Lammers, C.H.; Dettling, M. and Holsboer, F. (1994). Age-associated changes of pituitary-adrenocortical hormone regulation in humans: Importance of gender. *Neurobiology of Aging,* 15, 227-231.

Highly, J.D., Mehlman, P.T., Poland, R.E., Taub, D.M., Vickers, J., Soumi, S. and Linnoila, M. (1996). CSF Testosterone and 5-HIAA correlate with different types of aggressive behaviors. *Biological Psychiatry,* 40, 1067-1082.

Irwin, H.J. (1998). Attitudinal predictors of dissociation: Hostility and powerlessness. *Journal of Psychology,* 132 (4), 389-400.

Kaplan, M.L., Erensaft, M., Sanderson, W.C., Wetzler, S., Foote, B. and Asnis, S.

(1998). Dissociative symptomatology and aggressive behavior. Comprehensive Psychiatry, 39 (5), 271-276.

Konner, M. (1982). Biological aspects of the mother-infant bond. In: Emde, R.N., and Harmon, R.J. (eds.). *The development of Attachment and Affiliative Systems.* Plenum, New York.

Koolhaas, J.M., Meerlo, P., De Boer, S.F., Strubbe, J.H., and Bohus, B. (1997). The temporal dynamics of the stress response. *Neuroscience and Biobehavioral Reviews.* 21, 775-782.

Lewis, D.O. (1992). From abuse to violence: Psychophysiological consequences of maltreatment. *Journal of the American Academy of Child and Adolescent Psychiatry,* 31, 383-91.

Linnoila, M. (1996). CSF Testosterone and 5-HIAA correlate with different types of aggressive behaviors. *Biological Psychiatry,* 40, 1067-1082.

Mason, J.W., Giller, E.L. Jr., Kosten, T.R. and Wahby V.S. (1990). Serum testosterone levels in posttraumatic stress disorder inpatients. *Journal of Traumatic Stress,* 3 (3), 449-457.

Mattes, J.A. (1990). Comparative effectiveness of carbamezapine and propranolol for rage outbursts. *Journal of Neuropsychiatry and Clinical Neuroscience,* 2, 159-164.

Mayer, A.D., Monroy, M.A. and Roseblatt, J.S. (1990). Prolonged estrogen-progesterone treatment of nonpregnant ovariectomized rats: Factors stimulating home-cage and maternal aggression and short-latency maternal behavior. *Hormones and Behavior,* 24, 342-364.

McEwen, B.C. (1987). Gonadal and adrenal steroids and the brain: Implications for depression. In: Halbreich, U., ed. *Hormones and depression.* New York: Raven Press, 239-253.

Michelson, D. & Gold, P.W. (1994). Stress Responsive neurohormones in Depression and Anxiety. In: Den Boer, J.A. & Sitsen, J.M.A. (eds.). *Handbook of depression and anxiety: A biological approach.* Marcel Dekker.

Nielsen, D.A., Goldman, D., Virkkunen, M., Tokola, R., Rawlings, R. and Linnoila, M. (1994). Suicidality and 5-hydroxyindoleactetic acid concentration associated with tryptophan hydroxylase polymorphism. *Archives of General Psychiatry,* 51, 34-38.

Patchev, V.K., Hayashi, S., Orikasa, C. and Almeida O.F.X. (1995). Implications of estrogen-dependent brain organization for gender differences in hypothalamo-pituitary-adrenal regulation. *FASEB Journal,* 9, 419-423.

Rainey, J.M., Aleem, A., Oritz, A., Yaragani, V., Pohl, R. and Berchow, R. (1987). Laboratory procedure for the inducement of flashbacks. *American Journal of Psychiatry,* 144, 1317-1319.

Reeves, A. and Plum, F. (1969). Hyperphagia, rage, and dementia accompanying a ventromedial hypothalamic neoplasm. *Archives of Neurology,* 20, 229-234.

Reite, M. and Field, T. (eds.) (1985). *The psychobiology of attachment and separation.* Orlando, Florida: Academic Press.

Sano, K., Mayanagi, Y., Sekino, H., Ogashiwa, M. and Ishijima, B. (1970). Results of stimulation and destruction of the posterior hypothalamus in man. *Journal of Neurosurgery,* 33, 689-707.

Scarpa, A. and Raine, A. (1997). Psychophysiology of anger and violent behavior. *Psychiatric Clinics of North America,* 20 (2), 375-394.

Sheard, M.H. (1984). Clinical pharmacology of aggressive behavior. *Clinical Neuropharmacology,* 7, 173-183.

Stratakis, C.A. and Chrousos, G.P. (1994). Neuroendocrinology and pathophysiology of the stress system, *Annals of the New York Academy of Sciences,* 746, 1-18.

Sussman, E.J., Inoff-German, G., Loriaux, D.L., Cutler, G.B., and Chrousos, G. P. (1987). Hormones, emotional dispositions, and aggressive attributes in young adolescents. *Child Development,* 58: 1114-1134.

Squire, L.R. (1987). Memory and the brain, Oxford University Press, New York.

Tennes, K. (1982). The role of hormones in mother-infant transactions. In: Emde, R.N., and Harmon, R.J. (eds.). *The Development of Attachment and Affiliative Systems.* Plenum, New York, 75-80.

United States Department of Justice. (1977, 1980-1990). Uniform crime reports. *Crime in the United States.* Washington DC.

Van der Kolk, B.A., Greenberg, M.S., Boyd, H. and Krystal, J. (1985). Inescapable shock, neurotransmitters and addiction to trauma: Towards a psychobiology of post-traumatic stress. *Biological Psychiatry,* 20, 314-325.

Van der Kolk, B.A. and Saporta J. (1993). Biological response to psychic trauma. In: J.P. Wilson and B. Raphael, *International handbook of traumatic stress syndromes.* Plenum Press Series, 25-33.

Virkkunen, M., Goldman, D., Nielsen, D.A. and Linnoila, M. (1995). Low brain serotonin turnover rate (low CSF 5-HIAA) and impulsive violence. *Journal of psychiatry and neuroscience,* 20 (4), 271-275.

Yates, W.R., Perry, P. and Murry, S. (1992). Aggression and hostility in anabolic steroid users. *Biological Psychiatry,* 31, 1232-1234

Yehuda, R., Giller, E., Southwick, S., Lowy, M. and Mason, J. (1991). Hypothalamic-pituitary-adrenal dysfunction in posttraumatic stress disorder. *Biological Psychiatry,* 30, 1031-1048.

Zeman, W. and King, F. (1958). Tumors of the septum pellucidum and adjacent structures with abnormal affective behavior: An anterior midline structure syndrome. *Journal of Nervous and Mental Disease,* 127, 490-502.

Social Information Processed Self-Perceived Aggression in Relation to Brain Abnormalities in a Sample of Incarcerated Sexual Offenders

Reinhard Eher, MD
Martin Aigner, MD
Stefan Fruehwald, MD
Patrick Frottier, MD
Christine Gruenhut, MD

SUMMARY. In a sample of incarcerated sexual offenders, violent sexual behavior was found to be associated with a general impulsive and aggressive lifestyle and often times this was a sequel of a criminal socialization with nonsexual violent felonies in the past. Magnetic resonance tomography could detect numerous abnormalities in those offenders who were most violent. Offenders with brain abnormalities could be found to exhibit differences in processing social cue reading and emotions. In offenders without brain abnormalities self-perceived aggression was found to be triggered by social unassertiveness and avoidance, and was found to be negatively associated with interactional

Reinhard Eher, Martin Aigner, Stefan Fruehwald, Patrick Frottier, and Christine Gruenhut, are affiliated with the Department of Social Psychiatry, University Medical School Vienna, Waehringer Guertel 18-20, A-1090 Vienna, Austria. Justizanstalt Wien-Mittersteig, A-1050 Vienna, Austria.

Address correspondence to Reinhard Eher, MD, Department of Social Psychiatry, University Medical School Vienna, Waehringer Guertel 18-120, A-1090 Vienna, Austria (E-mail: reinhard.eher@univie.ac.at).

[Haworth co-indexing entry note]: "Social Information Processed Self-Perceived Aggression in Relation to Brain Abnormalities in a Sample of Incarcerated Sexual Offenders." Eher et al. Co-published simultaneously in *Journal of Psychology & Human Sexuality* (The Haworth Press, Inc.) Vol. 11, No. 3, 2000, pp. 37-47; and: *Sexual Offender Treatment: Biopsychosocial Perspectives* (ed: Eli Coleman, and Michael Miner) The Haworth Press, Inc., 2000, pp. 37-47. Single or multiple copies of this article are available for a fee from The Haworth Document Delivery Service [1-800-342-9678, 9:00 a.m. - 5:00 p.m. (EST). E-mail address: getinfo@haworthpressinc.com].

© 2000 by The Haworth Press, Inc. All rights reserved.

anxiety. No such interrelations could be found in the brain abnormality group. A deficient social cue reading processing in offenders exhibiting multisite brain abnormalities is hypothesized. *[Article copies available for a fee from The Haworth Document Delivery Service: 1-800-342-9678. E-mail address: getinfo@haworthpressinc.com <Website: http://www.haworthpressinc.com>]*

KEYWORDS. Sex offenders, brain abnormalities, violence

INTRODUCTION

There has been a long discussion about whether brain damage might lead to deviant sexual behavior. Only when computer tomography (CT) was introduced in 1973 and resulted in an increase in resolution of brain structure brain abnormality studies could be conducted reliably. Research, therefore, was no longer reliant on single case studies. Lanegvin et al. (1990) was one of the first doing CT research with samples of sexual offenders. However, although there was a series of studies conducted by this research group, results remained contradictory and no clear association between a specified brain region and a distinct paraphilia could be found.

Until now, about 15 computer tomography (CT), positron emission tomography (PET) and magnetic resonance imaging (MRI) studies investigating offender populations were conducted (Raine, 1993, 1997). Results of the most important studies concerning sexual offenders will be outlined as follows (see also Table 1): Hucker et al. (1986) could show that pedophiles exhibited significantly more abnormalities compared to normal controls. Pedophiles showed a significantly greater incidence of left and bilateral temporal lobe abnormalities (dilatation of the anterior temporal horns of the lateral ventricles). Langevin et al. (1988) compared incest offenders and nonviolent property offender groups. No differences in brain abnormality incidence between incest offenders and the property offender group could be found. Incest offenders having a history of violence on the other hand showed significantly more temporal lobe abnormalities than those without a history of violence (Langevin et al., 1988).

Hucker et al. (1988) conducted a study showing that sexual sadists had significantly more right-sided temporal horn abnormalities compared to nonsadists and controls. But "sadism" in this study was simply used for a violent sexual behavior, and, therefore abnormalities found could also be interpreted to be linked to a more violent behavior of offend-

TABLE 1. Sexual Offenders and Brain Abnormalities

Authors	Sample Characteristics	Results
Hucker, Langevin, Wirtzman, Bain, Handy, Chambers, and Wright (1986)	outpatient charged with a sexual assault on a minor (pedophilia) ■nonviolent nonsexuel property offenders	pedophiles (52% abnormalities) controls (17% abnormalities) *pedophiles showed a significantly greater incidence of left and bilateral temporal lobe abnormalities (dilatation of the anterior temporal horns of the lateral ventricels)*
Hucker, Langevin, Wortzman, Dickey, Bain, Handy, Chambers, and Wright (1988)	22 sadistic sexual assaulters ■21 non-sadistic sexual assaulters 36 nonviolent, nonsexual controls (property offenders)	sadists (41% right–sided temporal horn abnormalities) non–sadists (11% right–sided temporal horn abnormalities) controls (13%)
Langevin, Wortzman, Dickey, Wright, and Handy (1988)	91 incest offenders ■non violent property offenders	generalized CT abnormalities (not significant): offenders (24%) controls (30%) no difference in specific temporal lobe abnormalities *when incest offenders were divided in those with and without a history of violence:* violent (35% temporal lobe abnormalities) nonviolent (13% temporal lobe abnormalities)
Langevin, Wortzman, Wright, and Handy (1989a)	84 pedophiles ■32 property offenders	no significant group differences were observed for either general CT abnormalities or abnormalities specific to the temporal lobe
Langevin, Lang, Wortzman, Frenzel, and Wright (1989b)	15 exhbitionists 36 non-violent property offenders	no significant group differences were observed for either general CT abnormalities or abnormalities specific to the temporal lobe

ers. Langevin et al. could not find significant group differences for either general CT abnormalities or abnormalities specific to the temporal lobe between pedophiles and property offenders (1989a), and between exhibitionists and property offenders (1989b).

There are a few studies conducted with nonsexual offenders. Raine et al. (1997) investigated a sample of murderers by PET providing preliminary evidence about a network of abnormal cortical and subcortical brain processes that may predispose to violence. Also, data from Lapierre and Braun (1995) supported hypotheses about frontal lobe disfunctioning and its relationship both to psychopathy and violence. Psychopathic criminals in comparison to non-psychopathic criminals had impairments of performance on selected but not all neuropsychology tasks that measured frontal lobe activity. Golden et al. (1996) contended that the medial temporal lobe is often related to the disinhibition of anger and aggressive behaviors.

Raine (1993) suggested the hypothesis that there is a tendency for frontal dysfunction to be associated with violent offending (rape included), whilst temporal dysfunction is associated with sexual offending including incest and pedophilia. Empirical data, however, could not entirely support this hypothesis. Findings of CT, PET and MRI studies provide indications of a network of abnormal cortical and subcortical brain processes that may predispose to violence in general offenders as well as in sexual offenders leaving doubt about any specificity between changes in sexual functioning and a damage of any specified brain area.

Nevertheless, beside this strong empirical support about an association between violent and aggressive behavior and brain abnormalities in nonsexual and sexual offenders a key question concerns how these multisite deficits can translate into violence. Theories addressing classical conditioning and avoidance learning have been stressed trying to explain this question (Raine, 1993). Also, a social information-processing theory was provided hypothesizing a deficient or biased processing of social cue information. Dodge and Crick (1990) described a model that lays out a sequence of five cognitive operations involved in the development of aggressive behavior: encoding, interpretation, response search, response decision, and enactment. According to this model deficient processing would be predicted to lead to deviant social behavior and aggression.

Brain dysfunction, particularly lesions of the limbic system or the frontal cortex might interfere with the cognitive-emotional sequence involved in processing social cue information. The present study attempts to address the question of how social perceptions in sexual offenders are processed to emotionality and whether there can be found a different processing in an offender with and without brain abnormalities. Therefore, 38 incarcerated sexual offenders were investigated by magnetic resonance imaging (MRI) and subsequently asked to fill out questionnaires about aggressiveness and social perceptions. Our main hypothesis was that self-perception of aggressiveness is not linked to any social cue perception in high violent sexual offenders but is linked to social cue information in low violent offenders.

SUBJECTS

The population studied was comprised of thirty-eight imprisoned adult male sexual offenders. Mean age of offenders was 35.7 years

(SD = 12.9). Offenders had been charged previously to a prison sentence 2.9 (SD = 4.0) times for any offense. On average, offenders had been convicted previously 1.3 (SD = 1.3) times for a sexual offense, 1.2 (SD = 1.6) times for a nonsexual violent assault and 3.2 (SD = 3.4) times for a crime against property.

Diagnoses were set by experienced forensic psychiatrists according to DSM-IV criteria. The offenders met criteria of pedophilia, 8 (21%) 9 (23%) of sexual sadism; 23 (61%) had offended against adults, 15 (39%) had offended against minors.

METHOD

Magnetic Resonance Imaging (MRI)

Magnetic resonance tomography scans of the brain were performed with a 0.5 Tesla "circular polarized" scanner with a standard protocol with T2 weighted spin-echo sequences in axial plane. Slice thickness was 5 mm. All scans were visually inspected and reports were routinely provided by consultant neuroradiologists of the same institute. This ensured that the MRI scans were interpreted with the same consensus standards of normality used for a general patient population and not a standard special to psychiatric patients. All scan reports were in narrative format, and they were reviewed and coded according to presence or absence of brain abnormality. Neuroradiologists were blind to clinical diagnoses and offense history.

Violence Ratings

Offenders were distributed either to group I for "high violence" or group II for a "no or low violence." Violence ratings were undertaken according to proposals of Wong et al. (1984). We strictly orientated on the amount of overt aggression admitted no matter what might have been the intrapsychic reason for aggression. Therefore, we avoided to make our decisions upon implied intentions for aggression (e.g., expressive, instrumental, sadistic, . . .).

Measures

The *Inventory of Interpersonal Problems (IIP)*. The IIP (Alden et al., 1990, Horowitz et al., 1988, Horowitz et al., 1994) is comprised of the following eight subscales:

- *Domineering:* High scores on this scale reflect self-reported problems to accept others and problems according to controlling behavior.
- *Vindictive:* High scores on this scale reflect self-report on distrust of diminished capacity to assist others and a consummate will to avenge.
- *Cold:* High scores reflect self-report on a diminished capacity to love and empathize with others.
- *Socially Avoidant:* High scores reflect self-report on a lessened ability to self-disclose and connect with others.
- *Nonassertive:* High scores reflect self-report on a decreased ability to self-express constructively.
- *Exploitable:* High scores reflect self-report on the tendency to yield to the opinion of others and subsequently feel fleeced.
- *Overly Nurturant:* High scores reflect self-report on charitability and a tendency to enmesh with others.
- *Intrusive:* High scores reflect overly permeable personal boundaries and difficulties to self-regulate in interpersonal affairs.

The *Interactional Anxiety Questionnaire (IAF)*. The IAF (Becker, 1982, Becker, 1987) is comprised of a total of fifty-five items grouped in 8 eight scales. For the purpose of this study, the following five scales were used:

- *Fear of Assertion:* High scores reflect self-report of an inability to self-promote and comment upon the actions of others.
- *Fear of Negative Evaluation:* High scores reflect self-report of fearing the negative opinions of others.
- *Fear of Aggression:* High scores reflect self-report of fearing verbal and/or physical aggression.
- *Fear of Self Competence:* High scores reflect self-report on mistrusting one's own competence in situations where self-confidence is needed.
- *Fear of Violating Rules:* High scores reflect self-report of fearing situations where one has to violate social rules or personal boundaries.

Aggressiveness was measured by the *Inventory for the Assessment of Factors of Aggressiveness (FAF)*. The FAF (Hamper & Selg, 1975) is similar to the American Buss-Durkee Hostility Inventory (Buss & Durkee, 1957) and mainly concludes items related to hostility. Only the scales *Spontaneous Aggression* and *Reactive Aggression* were used in this study. Both subscales were added and comprised to the scale *Aggression*.

RESULTS

Findings of brain abnormalities by Magnetic Resonance Tomography

Regardless of location, 17 (44.7%) offenders had some structural brain abnormality. Four (10.5%) offenders had a cortical atrophy, one (2.6%) offender had periventricular lesions, six (15.8%) offenders had deep white matter lesions, one (2.6) offender had ventricular enlargements, and five (13.2%) offenders had multiple lesions.

Diagnoses actuarial variables and measures according to presence and absence of brain abnormalities

Groups did not differ significantly in terms of diagnoses, actuarial and measure variables. Violence was the only variable showing differences over groups near significance (($\chi2 = 3.27$, $p = 0.07$). Of the MRT negative group 47.6% had a high violent offense, whereas 76.5% of the brain abnormality group had a high violent offense. None of the measure variables (FAF, IIP, IAF) significantly differed over groups although there was a non-significant tendency of the brain abnormality group to show lower ratings in measures of aggression and anxiety.

Prediction of self-perceived aggression by perceptions of interpersonal problems and social support in relation to presence or absence of brain abnormalities

The correlation matrix for subscales of the IIP and IAF and self-perceived aggression (spontaneous and reactive aggressiveness) within both groups is shown in Table 2. A regression analysis identifying variables predicting aggressiveness was not performed due to the low sample number. IIP subscales Overly Nurturant and Exploitable correlated negatively and Socially Avoidant and Vindictiveness correlated

TABLE 2. Correlation of IIP and IAF scales with FAF scales (spontaneous and reactive aggression) according to presence and absence of brain abnormalities

	BA	non BA
	aggression	aggression
IIP		
Dominant	0.10	0.16
Vindictiveness	0.11	**0.48**
Cold	0.23	0.21
Social Avoidance	− 0.30	**0.56**
Nonassertive	− 0.24	0.19
Exploitable	− 0.12	− 0.61
Overly Nurturant	0.06	**− 0.70**
Intrusive	0.21	− 0.22
IAF		
Fear of Assertion	− 0.33	0.23
Fear of Negative Evaluation	0.31	− 0.10
Fear of Aggression	0.17	− 0.05
Fear of Self Competence	− 0.24	**0.48**
Fear of Violating Rules	− 0.28	**− 0.52**

Note. BA = offenders with MRT detected brain abnormalities, non BA = offenders without MRT detected brain abnormalities. Correlation coefficients greater then 0.50 are shown in bold.

positively with self-perceived aggression in the non brain abnormality group. Neither of the IIP subscales, however, significantly correlated with self-perceived aggression in the brain abnormality group. IAF subscales Fear of Violating Rules correlated negatively and Fear of Self Competence correlated positively with aggression in the group without brain anomlies. Neither of IAF subscales, on the one hand predicted aggression in the brain abnormality group.

DISCUSSION

There is a long discussion about how generalized brain dysfunction might predispose to violent or deviant behavior. Studies using different techniques have repeatedly shown that violent offenders have poorer brain functioning than control groups (Raine, 1993). In our study, however, we could also find an association between violent behavior and multisite brain deficits detected by MRI in incarcerated sexual offenders.

Although there is some empirical evidence about an association between violent behavior and brain dysfunction in both general criminals and sexual offenders, no clear theory could yet be strengthened by empirical data about how findings could be interpreted. Biosocial pathways have been discussed trying to explain key questions about how multisite deficits can translate into violence. Abnormalities located in the limbic system may relate to deficits in forming conditioned emotional responses and the failure to learn from experience. Prefrontal deficits, on the other hand, may lead to loss of self-control, impulsivity, or altered emotionality (Raine et al., 1997).

In our study, processing of self-perceived aggression according to social perceptions was studied in 38 incarcerated sexual offenders. In sexual offenders showing unspecified brain abnormalities self-perceived aggression could be shown not to be dependent from any social perception, neither from self-perception of social problems, nor from self-perception of social anxiety. In sexual offenders without brain abnormalities, on the other hand, self-perceived aggression was found to be linked to self-perceived social perceptions.

Violent and psychopathic behavior previously have been hypothesized to stem from a failure to process the emotional meaning of language, a deficit which was also called "semantic dementia" (Patrick et al., 1994). Psychopathic criminals have also been found to show an inability to anticipate the negative consequences of their own behavior by lacking the capability of an emotional imagery. In our study offenders exhibiting brain damages were found not to be able to link social cue information to self-perceptions of aggression and anxiety. Although both offender groups exhibited the same levels on IIP and IAF scales only those without brain abnormalities could link interpersonal perceptions to aggressiveness. A perception of feeling nurturing, being exploitable and fear of violating rules led to lower self-perception of aggressiveness. On the other hand, a feeling of being vindictive in relationships, as well as being socially avoidant led to higher levels of self-perceived aggressiveness in the sample without brain abnormalities.

Lack of empathy, callousness and manipulation reported for criminal psychopaths and violent offenders (Harris et al., 1994) might be a consequence of the disruption of social cue reading and feelings of aggression and anxiety. This disruption might be triggered–at least in some violent individuals–by minimal brain abnormalities.

Our data give some empirical evidence for an association between awareness and self-perception of social cues and self-perceived aggressiveness which is destroyed in those offenders exhibiting brain abnormalities. Thus, multisite brain deficits might translate into violence in interfering with a social processing sequence leading to a disruption of a social information-emotionality-chain. Nevertheless, one has to add that these result and their interpretations have to be interpreted cautiously due to small sample number and due to the lack of matched groups.

REFERENCES

Alden LE, Wiggins JS, Pincus AL. Construction of circumflex scales for the inventory of interpersonal problems. *Journal of Personality Assessment.* 1990; 55; 521-536.

Becker P. Towards a process analysis of test anxiety: Some theoretical and methodological observations. In: Schwarzer R, van der Ploeg H, Spielberger CD, eds. Advances in test anxiety research. Lisse: Swets & Zeitlinger; 1982.

Becker P. IAF-Interactions-Angst-Fragebogen (Interactional Anxiety Questionnaire), 2nd edition, Manual. Weinheim: Beltz; 1987.

Buss AH, Durkee A. An inventory for assessing different kinds of hostility. *Journal of Consulting and Clinical Psychology.* 1957; 21; 343-348.

Dodge KA, Crick NR. Social information processing bases of aggressive behavior in children. *Personality and Social Psychology Bulletin.* 1990; 16; 8-22.

Golden CJ, Jackson ML, Rohne AP, Gontkovsky ST. Neuropsychological correlates of violence and aggression: a review of the clinical literature. *Aggression Violent Behavior.* 1996; 1: 3-25.

Grant TH, Rice ME, Quinsey VL. Psychopathy as a taxon: Evidence that psychopaths are a discrete class. *Journal of Consulting and Clinical Psychology.* 1994; 62: 387-397.

Hampel R, Selg H. FAF-Fragebogen zur Erfassung von Aggressivitätsfaktoren (FAF-Inventory for the Assessment of Factors of Aggressiveness). Hogrefe: Goettingen; 1975.

Horowitz LM, Rosenberg SE, Bauer BA, Ureno G, Villasenor VS. Inventory of interpersonal problems: Psychometric properties and clinical applications. *Journal of Consulting and Clinical Psychology.* 1988; 56: 885-892.

Horowitz LM, Straub B, Kordy H. IIP-D-Inventar zur Erfassung Interpersonaler Probleme (Inventory of Interpersonal Problems)-Manual. Weinheim: Beltz; 1994.

Hucker S, Langevin R, Wortzman G, Bain J, Handy L, Chambers J, Wright S. Neuropsychological impairment in pedophiles. *Can Journal Behavioral Science.* 1986; 18: 440-448.

Hucker S, Langevin R, Wortzman G, Dickey R, Bain J, Handy L, Chambers J, Wright S. Cerebral damage and dysfunction in sexually aggressive men. *Annals of Sex Research.* 1988; 1: 33-47.

Langevin R, Lang RA, Wortzman G, Frenzel RR, Wright P. An examination of brain damage and dysfunction in genital exhibitionists. *Annals of Sex Research.* 1989b; 2: 77-94.

Langevin R, Wortzman G, Dickey R, Wright P, Handy L. Neuropsychological impairment in incest offenders. *Annals of Sex Research.* 1988; 1: 401-415.

Langevin R, Wortzman G., Wright P, Handy L. Studies of brain damage and dysfunction in sex offenders. *Annals of Sex Research.* 1989a; 2: 163-179.

Langevin R. Sexual anomalies and the brain. In: Marshall WL, Laws DR, Barbaree HE, eds. Handbook of the Sexual Assault. New York: Plenum Press; 1990: 103-113.

Lapierre D, Brain CM. Ventral frontal deficits in psychopathy: Neuropsychological test findings. Neuropsychologia 1995; 33: 139-151.

Patrick CJ, Cuthbert BN, Lang PJ. Emotion in the criminal psychopath: Fear image processing. *Journal of Abnormal Psychology.* 1994; 103: 523-534.

Raine A, Buchsbaum M, Lacasse L. Brain abnormalities in murderers indicated by positron emission tomography. *Bio Psychiatry.* 1997; 42: 495-508.

Raine A. The Psychopathology of Crime: Criminal Behavior as a Clinical Disorder. San Diego: Academic Press; 1993.

Wong MTH, Lumsden J, Fenton GW, Fenwick PBC. Electroencephalography, computed tomography and violence ratings of male patients in a maximum-security mental hospital. *Acta Psychiatric Scandinavia.* 1994; 90: 97-101.

Self-Concepts and Interpersonal Perceptions of Sexual Offenders in Relation to Brain Abnormalities

Stefan Fruehwald, MD
Reinhard Eher, MD
Patrick Frottier, MD
Martin Aigner, MD

SUMMARY. A higher rate of minimal brain abnormalities detected by Magnetic Resonance Imaging (MRI) is found in a sample of highly violent incarcerated sexual offenders compared to a low violent group. Although similar in age, the MRI-positive group (n = 17) exhibited more previous nonsexual violent felonies, and more offenses against property than the MRI-negative subjects (n = 21). When comparing self-perceptions of aggression, self-concepts and interpersonal problems in offender groups, those with brain abnormalities showed lower self-perceived aggression and slightly better self-concepts. Self-perceived-aggression in offenders without brain abnormalities was found to be highly dependent from social and interpersonal self perceptions, whereas these associations could not be shown in offenders with brain abnormalities. The preliminary conclusion is that minimal brain abnormalities in sexual offenders might lead to disruption of social perception and feelings of aggression and anxiety. This disconnection of a functioning feedback regulation between social perception and aware-

---

Stefan Fruehwald, Reinhard Eher, Patrick Frottier, and Martin Aigner are affiliated with the Department of Social Psychiatry, Vienna University Medical School, Vienna General Hospital, A-1090 Vienna, Austria (E-mail: stefan.fruehwald@ univie.ac.at).

[Haworth co-indexing entry note]: "Self-Concepts and Interpersonal Perceptions of Sexual Offenders in Relation to Brain Abnormalities." Fruehwald et al. Co-published simultaneously in *Journal of Psychology & Human Sexuality* (The Haworth Press, Inc.) Vol. 11, No. 3, 2000, pp. 49-56; and: *Sexual Offender Treatment: Biopsychosocial Perspectives* (ed: Eli Coleman, and Michael Miner) The Haworth Press, Inc., 2000, pp. 49-56. Single or multiple copies of this article are available for a fee from The Haworth Document Delivery Service [1-800-342-9678, 9:00 a.m. - 5:00 p.m. (EST). E-mail address: getinfo@haworthpress inc.com].

© 2000 by The Haworth Press, Inc. All rights reserved.

ness of social desirability and adequate feelings might be triggered by minimal brain abnormalities and thus be responsible for a more violent and less empathic behavior. *[Article copies available for a fee from The Haworth Document Delivery Service: 1-800-342-9678. E-mail address: getinfo@haworthpressinc.com <Website: http://www.haworthpressinc.com>]*

KEYWORDS. Sexual offenders, biological and psychosocial factors, self-concepts, aggression level, brain abnormalities

INTRODUCTION

In Forensic Psychiatry, new possibilities of assessing the dangerousness of Sex Offenders are being established. Traditionally, the probability of relapse was connected with criminal variables such as the violence of the actual offence (Rice 1991), the number of previous convictions (Hanson 1993), the time spent in custody (Rice 1991) or various traumatic events in the offender's childhood (Berner 1986). All of these parameters are undoubtedly important for the assessment of dangerousness, but none of them can be changed by therapy. A number of studies were published during the last years dealing with the relevance of changeable psychosocial factors (e.g., absence of denial and minimization, empathy for the victim, self-confidence, sensitivity, assertiveness, social competence in general) for the prediction of recidivism (Marshall 1994, Pithers 1994, Dwyer & Amberson 1989, Marshall & Barbaree 1989).

In the complex process of the beginning and maintenance of violent behavior, there was preliminary evidence presented for the predisposing relevance of certain brain abnormalities indicated by positron emission tomography (PET), computerized tomography (CT) and magnetic resonance imaging (MRI). Aigner et al. (1998) found a strong relationship between violence and unspecified brain abnormalities detected by MRI in a sample of 82 incarcerated male offenders. All these findings are to be considered preliminary today, as the proportion of biological, social, psychological, cultural, and situational factors is not yet understood (Raine 1997). Nevertheless, especially MRI as a high resolution brain imaging technique may broaden our knowledge of a possible neuroanatomical and neurophysiological basis of violent behavior (Raine 1993).

To our knowledge, no study has been conducted linking psychiatric, psychological, and criminological data with information yielded by modern brain imaging techniques like MRI. This approach might help to understand the relation between cognitive and emotional risk factors for violent offending upon the basis of neuroanatomical abnormalities. We investigated this possible correlation of minimal brain abnormalities with criminal history, self-concepts and the self-reported level of aggression.

METHOD

Ninety-five long-term incarcerated sex offenders were asked to answer a number of self-rating questionnaires, in order to evaluate characteristics of personality like self-concepts and interpersonal perceptions. These patients were inmates of a maximum security hospital for mentally disordered but guilty offenders in Vienna, Austria. The first instrument was the "FSKN" ("Frankfurt Scales of Self-Concepts") (Deusinger, 1986), assessing general performance, self-esteem, sensitivity, irritability and 6 other important components of self-concepts. The second instrument was the "FAF" ("Inventory for the Assessment of Factors of Aggressiveness") (Hampel & Selg, 1975), forming four scales to measure spontaneous and reactive aggression, excitability and inhibition of aggression. We also took demographic data (e.g., age), diagnosis, number of previous offenses, degree of violence of the last felony, length and method of therapy during custody, in order to find variables possibly influencing personal ideas and concepts of the self.

Ninety long-term incarcerated sex offenders were examined by MRI for possible brain abnormalities. All MRIs were done by the same laboratory and interpreted by experienced radiologists who were blinded to offenses and psychopathology. Patients suffering from schizophrenia, organic brain syndrome, and mental retardation were excluded in this study, in order to avoid any bias due to possible MRI-abnormalities caused by these illnesses in these patients. There were available both the results of the questionnaires and the MRIs for 38 offenders, the others were excluded here.

Offenders were divided into two groups with and without minimal brain abnormalities. The characteristics of these two groups were listed with regards to criminal history, psychiatric diagnosis and further information. A nonparametric analysis of variance tested group differences for each of the questionnaire subscales. Subsequently a correlation analysis was performed for the questionnaire scales subdivided for the two groups to detect correlations between the individual's self-percepted level of aggression and his self-concepts.

RESULTS

This sample was offenders that had been previously convicted on an average of more than 6 times and relapsed. They had been incarcerated 3.9 times; the length of the actual incarceration was 33.3 months. Most frequent psychiatric diagnoses were personality disorder (84%), alcohol addiction (66%), pedophilia (21%), and sexual sadism (24%). The majority of the offenders had been in analytic, systemic or behavior therapy.

Twenty-one (55%) of the offenders did not show minimal brain abnormalities, 17 (45%) did (Table 1). These two groups did not differ in age, total number of previous convictions, total number of sexual offences, psychiatric diagnosis personality disorder or alcohol abuse, but we found a higher number of offences against property (3.7 vs. 2.8 times) and a higher incidence of sexual sadism (29% vs. 19%) in the MRI-positive group.

Differences in self-concepts between offenders with and without brain abnormalities were near significance, showing the MRI-positive group to have better self-concepts. Differences in general problem-solving capacity (FSAL), sensitivity (FSEG) and the total score of self concepts (FSKN) reached significance-level. Self-perceived aggression did not differ in the two groups (Wilcoxon) (Table 2). Pearson's correlation analysis (Table 3) showed that the total score of self-concepts (FSKN) was negatively correlated with self-perceived aggression level (r = -0.49; p < 0.05) *only* in the *MRI-negative group,* whereas there was no correlation whatsoever in the MRI-positive group. In addition, there was found a significant correlation between self-perceived aggression and sensitivity (FSEG) (r = -0.47; p < 0.05), assertiveness towards others (FSST) (r = -0.54; p < 0.01), contact and relationship (FSKU) (r = -0.57; p < 0.01) and positive feedback by others (FSWA) (r = -0.53; p < 0.01) in the MRI-negative group: the higher the self-concepts, the lower the self-perceived aggression (and vice versa). On the other hand, patients with MRI abnormalities reported no correlating perceptions of self-concepts and aggression.

TABLE 1. Description of the sample

	total		MRI neg.		MRI pos.	
	n	%	n	%	n	%
n	38	100	21	55	17	45
Violent felony	26	68	14	67	12	71
Diagnosis: Pedophilia	8	21	4	19	4	24
Diagnosis: Sexual Sadism	9	24	4	19	5	29
Diagnosis: Exhibitionism	3	8	2	10	1	6
Diagnosis: Transvestitism/Fetishism	1	3	0	0	1	6
Diagnosis: Personality disorder	32	84	18	86	14	82
Alcohol abuse	25	66	13	62	12	71
	Mean	Std.dev.	Mean	Std.dev.	Mean	Std.dev.
Age (years)	35.7	13.0	35.9	12.8	35.4	13.5
Total number sexual offences against children	1.1	2.2	1.2	2.6	0.9	1.6
Total number sexual offences against adults	1.2	1.3	1.4	1.4	1.0	1.2
Total number violent offences	1.2	1.7	1.1	1.6	1.4	1.8
Total number offences against property	3.2	3.5	2.8	3.0	3.7	4.1
Total number previous convictions	6.4	4.8	6.2	4.6	6.6	5.2
Total number incarcerations	4.0	4.1	4.0	4.0	3.9	4.2
Time spent in Mittersteig (months)	33.3	42.1	30.6	31.2	36.7	53.7
Length of psychotherapy (months)	26.1	40.5	24.6	33.0	28.0	49.7

DISCUSSION

A relation between brain abnormalities and changes in personality and sexuality has been found by many researchers during the last years. Nevertheless it was not possible to link damages of specific brain regions to distinct psychological features or psychopathological symp-

TABLE 2. Results

	MRI neg.	MRI pos.	Wilcoxon
	n = 21	n = 17	
Aggression	8.09	6.50	ns
Total score/Self concepts FSKN	31 8.55	352.07	0.06
General performance FSAL	40.38	44.06	ns
General problem-solving capacity FSAP	43.00	48.12	0.05
Self confidence-decisions FSVE	24.43	26.37	ns
Self esteem FSSW	42.71	44.44	ns
Senslflvity FSEG	22.14	25.33	0.03
Assertiveness towards others FSST	48.14	54.07	ns
Contact and Relationship FSKU	24.95	26.06	ns
Positive feedback by others FSWA	24.00	22.62	ns
Irritability FSIA	22.76	24.81	ns
Feelings towards others FSGA	23.95	25.75	ns

toms. Brain mechanisms that underlie complex processes like criminal and violent behavior will involve multiple brain sites that form one or more neural networks which contribute to such behavior (Raine 1993). Similarly psychological attitudes like self-concepts, empathy, emotionality or mood may be results of well-functioning neural networks. It is a known fact that structural brain damage (e.g., stroke) causes not only physical disabilities, but also frequently leads to depressed mood (Starkstein & Robinson, 1989), cognitive impairment (Burvill et al., 1997), anxiety (Burvill et al., 1995) or other psychiatric disorders.

The lack of empathy reported for criminal psychopaths (Cleckley 1976) might be reflected by the disruption of social perception and feelings of aggression in the offender group with MRI-detected brain abnormalities in this study. This disconnection of a functioning feedback regulation between perception and awareness of social desirability and adequate feelings might be triggered by minimal brain abnormalities. Thus, neuroanatomical abnormalities detected in Magnetic Resonance Imaging might hinder better coping strategies and thus be re-

TABLE 3. Correlation analysis of "FSKN" subscales and self-perceived aggression				
	MRI neg. (n = 21)		MRI pos. (n = 17)	
	Aggression	p	Aggression	p
General performance FSAL	− 0.29		0.23	
General problem-solving capacity FSAP	− 0.39		0.14	
Self confidence-decisions FSVE	− 0.39		− 0.14	
Self esteem FSSW	− 0.11		0.22	
Sensitivity FSEG	− 0.47	*	− 0.13	
Assertiveness towards others FSST	− 0.54	**	0.01	
Contact and Relationship FSKU	− 0.57	**	0.25	
Positive feedback by others FSWA	− 0.53	**	− 0.03	
Irritability FSIA	− 0.40		− 0.26	
Feelings towards others FSGA	− 0.33		− 0.10	
Total score/Self concepts FSKN	− 0.48	*	− 0.01	

$* = p < .05; ** = p < .01$

sponsible for a more violent and less empathic behavior. Patients showing minimal MRI-abnormalities might therefore need special rehabilitational settings in forensic psychiatry.

Due to small sample numbers, lack of matched control groups (normal males, nonviolent offenders, nonviolent mentally ill male patients), and lacking information about the specifity of minimal brain damage, all results must be interpretated cautiously so far to avoid misleading conclusions.

Within the large number of psychological, social and cultural factors predisposing to violent behavior it is important to take into account both biological and psychological measurement in clinical research, at least from a viewpoint of relapse prevention. Finally we want to state again: Patients showing structural brain abnormalities could be understood as disabled and might need special treatment and rehabilitational facilities.

REFERENCES

Aigner, M., R. Eher, S. Fruehwald, P. Frottier, K. Gutierrez, S.M. Dwyer (1999). Brain Abnormalities and Violent Behavior. *Journal of Psychology and Human Sexuality.* In press.

Berner, W., E. Karlick-Bolten (1986). Verlaufsformen der Sexualkriminalität. Enke, Stuttgart.

Burvill, P.W., G. Johnson, K. Jamrozik, C. Anderson, E. Stewart-Wynne (1997). Risk factors for Post-Stroke Depression. *International Journal of Geriatric Psychiatry 12,* 219-226.

Burvill, P.W., G.A. Johnson, K.D. Jamrozik, C.S. Anderson, E.G. Stewart-Wynne, T.M.H. Chakera (1995). Anxiety Disorders after Stroke: Results from the Perth Community Stroke Study. *British Journal of Psychiatry 166,* 328-332.

Cleckley, H.C. (1976). The Mask of Sanity. 5th edition St. Louis: Mosby.

Deusinger, I (1986). FSKN-Die Frankfurter Selbstkonzeptskalen. Hogrefe-Verlag, Göttingen/Toronto/Züerich.

Dwyer, S.M., J.L. Amberson (1989). Behavioral Patterns and Personality Characteristics of 56 Sex Offenders: A Preliminary Study. *Journal of Psychology and Human Sexuality* 2(1), 105-117.

Hampel, R., H. Selg (1975). FAF-Fragebogen zur Erfassung von Aggessivitätsfaktoren. Hogrefe-Verlag, Göttingen/Toronto/Züerich

Hanson, R.K., R.A. Steffy, R. Gauthier (1993), Long-Term Recidivism of Child Molesters. *Journal of Consoling and Clinical Psychology,* 61 (4), 646-652.

Marshall, W.L. (1994). Treatment Effects on Denial and Minimization in Incarcerated Sex Offenders. *Behavior Research and Therapy 32 (5),* 559-564.

Marshall, W.L., H.E. Barbaree (1989). Outcome of Comprehensive Cognitive-Behavioral Treatment Programs. In: Laws, D.R. (Ed.): Relapse Prevention with Sexual Offenders, Guilford Press, New York.

Pithers, W.D. (1989). Relapse Prevention with Sexual Offenders. In Laws, D.R.(Ed.), Relapse Prevention with Sex Offenders. New York: Guilford Press.

Pithers, W.D. (1994). Process Evaluation of a Group Therapy Component designed to Enhance Sexual Offenders' Empathy for Sexual Abuse Survivors. *Behavior Research and Therapy 32 (5),* 565-570.

Raine, A., M. Buchsbaum, L. LaCase (1997). Brain Abnormalities in Murderers Indicated by Positron Emission Tomography. *Biological Psychiatry 42,* 495-508

Raine, A. (1993). The Psychopathology of Crime: Criminal Behavior as a Clinical Disorder. San Diego: Academic Press.

Rice, M.E., V.L. Quinsey, G.T. Harris (1991). Sexual Recidivism among Child Molesters Released from a Maximum Security Psychiatric Institution. *Journal of Consulting and Clinical Psychology 59 (3),* 381-386.

Starkstein, S.E., R.G. Robinson (1989). Affective Disorders and Cerebral Vascular Disease. *British Journal of Psychiatry 154,* 170-182.

Brain Abnormalities and Violent Behavior

Martin Aigner, MD
Reinhard Eher, MD
S. Fruehwald, MD
Patrick Frottier, MD
K. Gutierrez-Lobos, MD
S. Margretta Dwyer, PhD

ABSTRACT. *Introduction:* It is difficult to rationally discuss the question of whether violent behaviour is a disorder because violent actions engender very strong emotional reactions in the public. But there are good reasons to believe that a variety of social and biological factors predispose the individual toward criminal behaviour. This study concerns the question, whether there is an association between violent behaviour and brain abnormalities.

Method: Ninety-six mentally ill offenders of a high security prison consecutively underwent magnetic resonance imaging of the brain (MRI). The number of sex offenders was 62.5%. Fourteen offenders were excluded because they had a neurological disease, a psychotic disorder, a severe organic mental disorder or they were older than 60 years. All scan reports were in narrative format, and they were reviewed and coded according to presence or absence of brain abnormali-

Martin Aigner, Reinhard Eher, S. Fruehwald, Patrick Frottier and K. Gutierrez-Lobos are affiliated with the Department of Social Psychiatry, University of Vienna, A-1090 Vienna, Austria and Justizanstalt Wien-Mittersteig, A-1050 Vienna, Austria. S. Margretta Dwyer is Faculty Emeritus, at the Department of Family Practice and Community Health, University of Minnesota, Minneapolis and Forensic Consultant, MN, USA.

Address correspondence to M. Aigner, MD, Department of Social Psychiatry, University of Vienna, A-1090 (E-mail: Martin.Aigner@akh-wien.ac.at).

[Haworth co-indexing entry note]: "Brain Abnormalities and Violent Behavior." Aigner et al. Co-published simultaneously in *Journal of Psychology & Human Sexuality* (The Haworth Press, Inc.) Vol. 11, No. 3, 2000, pp. 57-64; and: *Sexual Offender Treatment: Biopsychosocial Perspectives* (ed: Eli Coleman, and Michael Miner) The Haworth Press, Inc., 2000, pp. 57-64. Single or multiple copies of this article are available for a fee from The Haworth Document Delivery Service [1-800-342-9678, 9:00 a.m. - 5:00 p.m. (EST). E-mail address: getinfo@haworthpressinc.com].

© 2000 by The Haworth Press, Inc. All rights reserved.

ty. Neuroradiologists were blind to clinical diagnoses and offence history. Offenders were distributed either to a "high violent group" or to a "no or low violent group." There was no significant difference in age between both groups.

Results: In the included sample (n = 82; 50 sex offenders) 48.8% had MRI abnormalities. In the high violent group 65.5% showed MRI abnormalities. In the low violent group 16.6% had MRI abnormalities. This difference is significant (p = 0.001). The high violent sex offender group showed a MRI abnormality rate of 59.4%, and the low violent sex offender group 22.2%. The difference is significant (p = 0.011). There is no significant difference in MRI abnormality rate between the sex offender and the "non sex offender."

Conclusions: The results indicate that there is an association between unspecified brain anomalies and high violent behaviour in the whole sample as well as in the sex offender group. There is no association between sexual offence and unspecified brain abnormalities. Modern brain imaging techniques such as magnetic resonance imaging should be included in the diagnostic procedure of mentally ill offenders. *[Article copies available for a fee from The Haworth Document Delivery Service: 1-800-342-9678. E-mail address: getinfo@haworthpressinc.com <Website: http://www.haworthpressinc.com>]*

KEYWORDS. Sex offender, Magnetic Resonance Imaging, violence, brain anomalies

INTRODUCTION

It is difficult to rationally discuss the question of whether violent behaviour is a disorder because violent actions engender very strong emotional reactions in the public. But new imaging techniques offer the promise of giving psychiatric evaluations of dangerousness and violence much greater objectivity (Tancredi and Volkow, 1988). Of cause, the violent behaviour of man is not a unitary phenomena. Besides complex concepts of social interaction, clinical and forensic factors for violent behaviour (Elliot, 1992; Torrey, 1994; Grubin, 1995), a biological or organic etiologic perspective might be promising (Dolan, 1994).

Neurobiological disorders are amazingly common among criminal defendants (Simon, 1996). In a variety of psychiatric disorders magnetic resonance imaging (MRI) abnormalities of the brain could be assessed (Woods, 1995). Brain abnormalities may impair cognitive, affective and social functions, and this may be a risk factor for violent behaviour. The capacity for aggression and its control is vested in an excitatory and inhibitory system situated in the orbitofrontal cortex, septal area, amygdala, caudate, thalamus, hypothalamus, raphe nuclei, cortex of the anterior lobe of the cerebellum, and elsewhere in the "limbic system," with the neocortex, especially the dorsolateral pre-frontal regions (Bradshaw and Mattingley, 1995; Volavka, 1995). But researchers need to move away from overly simplistic notions of linking one specific brain region to criminal and violent behaviour. Brain mechanisms that underlie criminal and violent behaviour will involve multiple brain sites that form one or more neural networks which contribute to such behaviour (Raine, 1993).

This study concerns the question, whether there is an association between violent behaviour and brain abnormalities.

METHOD

Mentally ill offenders (n = 96) of a high security prison consecutively underwent magnetic resonance imaging of the brain (MRI). All MRIs were visually inspected and reports were routinely provided by a consultant neuroradiologist. The violence ratings were rated blind to the MRI reports. The number of sex offenders was 62.5%. Fourteen offenders were excluded because they had a neurological disease, a psychotic disorder, a severe organic mental disorder or they were older than 60 years.

All scan reports were in narrative format, and they were reviewed and coded according to presence or absence of brain abnormality. Offenders were distributed either to a "high violent group" or to a "no or low violent group." Eighty-two male offenders were rated according their violent behaviour as high violent and moderate or low violent. Violence ratings were undertaken according to proposals of Marshall (1994), Wong et al. (1993) and Prentky and Knight (1991). We strictly oriented on the amount of overt aggression admitted no matter what might have been the intrapsychic reason for aggression. Therefore, we avoided to make our decisions upon implied intentions for aggression (e.g., expressive, instrumental, sadistic,. . .). Criteria for distribution for either group I or group II are listed in Table 1. There was no significant difference in age between MRI positive and MRI negative group within the general sample and within the sex offenders (Table 2).

RESULTS

In the included sample (n = 82) 48.8% exhibited MRI abnormalities. In the sex offender group (n = 50) 46.0% exhibited MRI abnormalities (see Tables 3 and 4).

TABLE 1. Violence Rating

low violent group	high violent group
1. exhibitionism 2. verbal coercion 3. forced sex without directly injuring the victim 4. had tried to commit rape or other offence but had withdrawn because of victim's resistance	1. aggressive sexual assault with vaginal or anal penetration 2. directly severely injuring the victim by applying physical force 3. homicide 4. fire setting

TABLE 2. Sample–Age

		MRI 0	MRI 1	T-Test
Sample	n = 82	40	42	
Age: Mean	35.83	33.9	37.7	n.s.
(SD)	(9.99)	(10.06)	(9.70)	
Sex offender	n = 50	27	23	
Age: Mean	37.16	35.4	39.2	n.s.
(SD)	(10.66)	(10.47)	(9.60)	

MRI 0: group with no brain abnormality

MRI 1: group with brain abnormality

TABLE 3. MRI findings and violent behaviour

Author	Year	MRI	n	Key findings
Tonkonogy	1991	MRI	14 violent OBS	5 cases with anterior-inferior temporal lobe
		/CT	9 nonviolent OBS	lesions in violent group
Aigner et al. (this study)	1998	MRI	82 male offenders (50 sex offenders)	high violent group: 65.5% MRI abnormalities low violent group: 16.6% MRI abnormalities difference is significant ($\chi2 = 16.214$, DF = 1, p = 0.0001)

OBS: organic brain syndrome

TABLE 4. MRI abnormality–Rate

	Sample	High violent	Low violent	p-value
Sample (n = 82)	48.8%	65.5%	16.6%	p = 0.001
Sex offender (n = 50)	46.0%	59.4%	22.2%	p = 0.011

In the high violent group 65.5% showed MRI abnormalities. In the low violent group 16.6% had MRI abnormalities. This difference was significant ($\chi^2 = 16.214$, DF = 1, p = 0.001). The high violent sex offender group showed a MRI abnormality rate of 59.4%, and the low violent sex offender group 22.2%. The difference was significant ($\chi^2 = 6.402$, DF = 1, p = 0.011). No significant difference was found in MRI abnormality rate between the sex offender and the "non sex offender" (22.0% vs. 39.0%; $\chi^2 = 2.805$, DF = 1, p = 0.094).

Temporal abnormalities alone (n = 3) were exclusively found in high violent sexual offenders with sexual sadism. Cortical atrophy–especially frontal–were only found in the high violent group.

DISCUSSION

Since the mid-1970s computed tomography was the first of a cascade of new approaches to visualizing the structure and function of the brain. Computerized brain imaging (CT, MR, SPECT and PET) has redrawn much of psychiatry's landscape. Schizophrenia, dementias and even neurotic disorders such as obsessive compulsive disorders, as well as childhood developmental disorders have revealed abnormalities on brain imaging (Lewis and Higgins, 1996). Brain abnormalities and their association with changes in personality and sexuality have also been discussed for many years. In the diagnostic processes of mentally ill offenders, these imaging techniques have been used to a greater extent. Evidence could be found by several investigators for an occurrence of sexual aggressiveness and specific temporal horn dilatations detected by computed tomography (Langevin et al., 1990). Considerable brain anomalies have also been described to be associated with general purposeless violent behaviour (Volkow 1987, Dolan 1994) in a general psychiatric population as well as with a tendency of committing more violent crimes in a mentally ill offender population (Wong 1994).

This is in accordance with our study, that shows a significant higher brain abnormality rate in the high violent offender group. This high abnormality rate seems to be specificly associated with high violence. There is no difference in abnormality rate between sex offenders and "non-sex offenders."

When multiple brain anomalies were excluded, cortical atrophy was only found in the high violent group in this study. This finding is in concordance with findings of Volkow and Tancredi (1987), who described psychiatric patients with repetitive purposeless violent behaviour showing generalized cortical atrophy. Wong et al. (1994) and Langevin (1985) reported a very high incidence of abnormalities localized to temporal regions in a violent population (41% in a general violent population and 56% of sadistic sexual aggressives). All our exclusive temporal horn abnormalities were found in sadistic sex offenders. Miller et al. (1997) compared patients with fronto-temporal dementia and patients with Alzheimer's disease. Their study supports a relationship between fronto-temporal dysfunction and disruptive and aggressive social behaviour. Mentally ill offenders with concomitant violence were significantly more likely to have lesions in the anterior-inferior temporal lobe than those without violence (Tonkonogy, 1991).

Preliminary findings of murderers pleading not guilty by reason of insanity showed reduced glucose metabolism in the prefrontal cortex, superior parietal gyrus, left angular gyrus, and the corpus callosum, while abnormal asymmetries of activity (left hemisphere lower than right) were also found in the amygdala, thalamus, and medial temporal lobe. These areas may be part of a network of abnormal cortical and subcortical brain processes that may predispose to violence (Raine et al., 1997).

Taken together, the results of this study indicate that there is an association between unspecified brain anomalies and high violent behaviour in the whole sample as well as in the sex offender group. The basis for diagnosis of such dramatic forms of behavioral disorders should therefore include modern brain imaging techniques such as magnetic resonance imaging in order to allow patients appropriate treatment and legal protection. With MRI more specific quantitative evaluation of structural abnormalities and more sensitive detection of lesions have been possible.

Like unspecified damages of a hologram lead to an "unsharp picture," unspecified brain damages may represent a factor for "rough" behaviour. Further, the frontal and frontoparietal cortex and periventricular limbic regions may represent core structures of neural networks which contribute to high violent behaviour. In this study there was found no association between sexual offence and unspecified brain abnormalities. But the temporal region seems to be a core structure of neural networks which might contribute to sadistic sexual behaviour.

This study cannot be taken to demonstrate that violence is determined by brain abnormalities alone, nor does it demonstrate that MRI can be used as a diagnostic technique for violent behaviour.

REFERENCES

Bradshaw J.L. and Mattingley J.B. Clinical Neuropsychology. Behavioral and Brain Science. 1995; Academic Press, San Diego, Boston, New York, London, Sydney, Tokyo, Toronto.

Dolan M. Psychopathy-A Neurobiological Perspective. *Brit. J. Psychiatry.* 1994; 165:151-159.

Elliot F.A. Violence. The neurological contribution: An overview. *Archives of Neurology.* 1992; 49:595-603.

Grubin D. Sexual murder. *Br. J. Psychiatry.* 1994; 165:624-629.

Langevin R. Sexual Anomalies and the Brain. In W.L. Marshall, D.R. Laws, & H.E. Barbaree (Eds.), Handbook of the sexual assault 1990; pp. 103-113. New York: Plenum Press.

Lewis S. and Higgins N. Brain Imaging in Psychiatry. 1996; Blackwell Science Ltd., Oxford, London, Edinburgh.

Marshall W.L. Treatment effects on denial and minimization in incarcerated sex offenders. *Behavior Research and Therapy.* 1994; 32, 559-564.

Miller B.L., Darby A., Benson D.F., Cummings J.L. and Miller M.H. Aggressive, socially disruptive and antisocial behaviour associated with fronto-temporal dementia. *Br. J. Psychiatry.* 1997; 170: 150-155.

Raine A. The Psychopathology of Crime. Criminal Behavior as a Clinical Disorder. 1993; Academic Press, San Diego, New York, Boston.

Raine A., Buchsbaum M. and LaCasse L. Brain abnormalities in murderers indicated by positron emission tomography. *Biol. Psychiatry.* 1997; 42: 495-508.

Prentky R.A., and Knight R.A. Identifying critical dimensions for discrimination among rapists. *Journal of Consulting and Clinical Psychology.* 1991; 59, 643-661.

Simon R.I. Bad Men Do What Good Men Dream. 1996; American Psychiatric Press, Inc. Washington, London.

Tancredi L.R. and Volkow N. Neural substrates of violent behaviour: Implications for law and public policy. *Int. J. Law and Psychiatry.* 1988; 11:13-49.

Tonkonogy J.M. Violence and temporal lobe lesion: Head CT and MRI data. *J. Neuropsychiatry* 1991; 3:189-196.

Torrey EF. Violent behaviour by individuals with serious mental illness. Hosp. Community Psychiatry. 1994; 45:653-662.

Volavka J. Neurobiology of Violence. 1995; American Psychiatric Press, Inc. Washington, London.

Volkow N.D., & Tancredi L. Neural substrates of violent behavior. A preliminary study with positron emission tomography. *British Journal of Psychiatry.* 1987; 151, 668-673.

Wong M.T.H., Lumsden J., Fenton G.W., & Fenwick P.B.C. Electroencephalography, computed tomography and violence ratings of male patients in a maximum-security mental hospital. *Acta Psychiatrica Scandinavia.* 1994; 90, 97-101.

Wong M., Lumsden J., Fenton G., & Fenwick P. Violence rating of special hospital patients. *Journal of Forensic Psychiatry.* 1993; 4, 471-480.

Woods B.T., Brennan S., Yurgelun-Todd D., Young T., and Panzarino P. MRI abnormalities in major psychiatric disorders: An exploratory comparative study. *J Neuropsychiatry Clin Neurosci.* 1995; 7:49-53.

The Treatment
of Adult Male Child Molesters
Through Group Family Intervention

Dorothy W. Walker, MS

ABSTRACT. This paper explores the effectiveness of treating the child molester in multiple contexts as opposed to in-group therapy alone. Research indicates that sexual abuse may stem from a combination of family dysfunction (Hanson et al., 1994) and further, that family members' decisions impact the therapeutic process (Lipovsky, 1991). These and other findings suggest that effective counseling of sexual offenders should include not only the perpetrator, but the family members as well. This paper outlines a current treatment program utilizing a group process of relapse prevention and cognitive behavioral therapy techniques in concert with a companion group for partners and a therapeutic nursery for preschool-aged children. Using archival data, this paper

Dorothy W. Walker is Director of the Sexual Offender Treatment Program (SOTP). She is a Clinical Member of the Association for the Treatment of Sexual Abusers (ATSA). Recently she has been asked to participate in a Sex Offender Control Task Force, appointed by the North Carolina Department of Corrections, Division of Adult Probation/Parole, to help develop a comprehensive strategy for the management of sex offenders. She has been treating adult male child molesters for eight years.

Address correspondence to Dorothy W. Walker, Exchange/SCAN, 500 West Northwest Boulevard, Winston-Salem, NC 27105.

The author would like to acknowledge George Bryan, Jr., the Director of Stop Child Abuse Now (SCAN), Kimberly Brindle, Gerald Allen, and Jann Briscoe for their comments on a previous version of this manuscript. The author thanks Eli Coleman and Michael H. Miner for their comments on an earlier draft of this paper.

This paper is based on research presented at the Fifth International Conference on the Treatment of Sex Offenders, Caracas, Venezuela, March 24, 1998.

[Haworth co-indexing entry note]: "The Treatment of Adult Male Child Molesters Through Group Family Intervention." Walker, Dorothy W. Co-published simultaneously in *Journal of Psychology & Human Sexuality* (The Haworth Press, Inc.) Vol. 11, No. 3, 2000, pp. 65-73; and: *Sexual Offender Treatment: Biopsychosocial Perspectives* (ed: Eli Coleman, and Michael Miner) The Haworth Press, Inc., 2000, pp. 65-73. Single or multiple copies of this article are available for a fee from The Haworth Document Delivery Service [1-800-342-9678, 9:00 a.m. - 5:00 p.m. (EST). E-mail address: getinfo@haworthpressinc.com].

© 2000 by The Haworth Press, Inc. All rights reserved.

addresses the effectiveness of the program and highlights the usefulness of involving family members in the process. *[Article copies available for a fee from The Haworth Document Delivery Service: 1-800-342-9678. E-mail address: getinfo@haworthpressinc.com <Website: http://www.haworthpressinc. com>]*

KEYWORDS. Sexual offenders, child molesters, treatment, family

Treating sexual offenders involves difficulties not encountered when treating clients with other presenting concerns, not the least of which is the fact that sexual offenders don't always want to be treated and frequently deny that they have a problem. Because of this disposition, treatment professionals must carefully plan strategies that challenge cognitive distortions and counter denial, while seeking to modify behavior. The literature that evaluates the effectiveness of treatment programs for sexual offenders suggests that family involvement is key to working through the denial and distortion and leads to a more positive outcome (Silovsky & Hembre-Kiger, 1994; Knopp, 1982; Borduin et al., 1990; Henggeler, 1997; Lipovsky, 1991; Lockhart et al., 1989; Roesler et al., 1993; Henderson et al., 1989; Hansen et al., 1994; Abbott, 1995).

In the Sexual Offender Treatment Program (SOTP), based in North Carolina, counselors have also recognized the need to examine the role of the family in the treatment process. Over the years we noted that those men whose families were actively involved with treatment tended to stay in treatment and appeared to receive greater benefit. While this program does not utilize a strict family systems approach as espoused by Minuchin (1985) or Bowen (1985; but compared to Haley, 1985; and Weakland, 1985), the overarching philosophy of the systems approach is embraced by the program, according to Skynner, (1981).

> A systems approach does not necessarily involve bringing people into physical proximity, through working with actual groups. . . , the essential feature lies in the therapist's awareness and attitude, whereby he never gets completely lost in detail but constantly remembers, with part of his mind, the interconnectedness of the whole–individuals, family and community. (p. 49)

This is nearer to the philosophy that has evolved as the SOTP has progressed. While counselors involved with the SOTP do not regularly provide structured family therapy we do solicit the input of family members, provide treatment programming for the offender's partners, and provide therapy to other pre-school aged children who reside in the home where abuse has taken place. In addition, there are a number of informal family related services that are provided on an individual basis dependent upon family need (i.e., family meetings, couples meetings, provision of educational information, mediation, and referral).

The idea of a treatment program began in 1990 as a result of community concern for the ever increasing number of child sexual abuse cases originating in Forsyth County. The program was initiated by a community task force that sought to provide services for men who were circumventing the justice system. The SOTP program is a treatment program utilizing a group process of relapse prevention and cognitive behavioral therapy techniques (treatment modalities found to be associated with lower recidivism rates; see Marshall & Pithers, 1994; and Alexander, 1993) in concert with a companion group for partners, a therapy group for adult female incest survivors and a therapeutic nursery for preschool-aged children.

This study examines the effectiveness of SOTP in treating sex offenders. In particular, the study assesses whether involving others in the treatment process is associated with increased probability of remaining in therapy and lower recidivism rates. The study also looks for other possible correlates of successful therapy.

DATA

Participants

Archival data for 106 males who have entered the SOTP program since 1990 are reported here. The mean age for the men was 36 years with a range from 18 to 69 years. The majority of men, 84 (79.2%) were white; 14 (13.2%) were African-American; 5 (4.7%) were Mexican; and 3 (2.7%) were of other Latino or Native American descent. Sixty-four (60.4%) of the men were married; 23 (21.7%) were divorced; and 18 (17.0%) were single. The average education level was a high school degree. Thirty-eight (35.8%) of the men had less than a high school degree, while 22 (20.7%) of them had attended college.

Variables

There were two criterion variables of interest. The first was treatment disposition: Whether the client successfully completed treatment, left treatment (left voluntarily, was dismissed or transferred, or was reincarcerated), or was still in treatment. Whether or not the person reoffended was also recorded. A conviction, by the court, of a second offense was recorded as a reoffense.

Several predictor variables were examined to see if they were related to the outcome measures. Those of primary interest included whether or not a family member was involved at all with treatment; which family member was involved; how the family member was involved (e.g., telephone calls or personal visits with the counselors, individual or group therapy); and what assistance the family member provided (e.g., accompanying the offender to therapy, providing information on the family situation, giving family history, monitoring and reporting the offender's behavior.) Several demographic variables were examined, including age, race/ethnicity, education level, income level, and marital status. Finally, the relation of the offender to the victim and the type of offense were recorded.

RESULTS

Disposition

To test the hypothesis that family involvement was associated with treatment disposition (left treatment, completed treatment, still in treatment), a chi-squared analysis was performed. For the purpose of this analysis, involvement was defined as any act by a family member or significant other that was related to therapy.[1] By this standard, the families of roughly half of the men in treatment were involved. As expected, whether or not the family was involved was related to treatment disposition, $\chi^2 (2) = 5.53$, $p = .06$. As an aid to interpreting the relationship between disposition and family involvement, the tau statistic was computed. For this analysis, * = .03. We can interpret this value as the proportion of variation in disposition that is explained by family involvement.[2]

Table 1 shows the relationship between family involvement and treatment disposition for the men in the program. In this table, the "Left Treatment" disposition category is further subdivided for clari-

TABLE 1. Frequencies for family involvement by treatment disposition*

Count (row %)	completed treatment	dismissed	withdrew	removed incarcerated	transfer	still in treatment	Row Total
family not Involved	9 (17.3%)	7 (13.5%)	12 (23.1%)	10 (19.2%)	7 (13.5%)	7 (13.5%)	52 (49.1%)
family Involved	12 (22.2%)	3 (5.6%)	7 (13.0%)	7 (13.0%)	9 (16.7%)	16 (29.6%)	54 (50.9%)
Colnnm Total	21 (19.8%)	10 (9.4%)	19 (17.9%)	17 (16.0%)	16 (15.1%)	23 (21.7%)	106 (100%)

* The "dismissed" category refers to people who were dismissed from the program because of lack of progress. The "withdrew" category refers to those who left voluntarily. Three people in the "removed/incarcerated" category were deported from the country; the rest were incarcerated. The "transfer" category refers to people who transferred to other programs, usually because of relocation.

fication. As can be seen from the table, when the family was involved, the men were more likely to complete treatment or to remain in treatment. Men whose families were involved were less likely to be dismissed for lack of progress, to withdraw voluntarily, or to be re-incarcerated.

Type of involvement was also examined for any relationship to treatment outcome. Whether or not family members had conferences with the therapist was unrelated to disposition, $\chi^2(2) = 0.14$, n.s. ($\tau = .001$). Accompanying the offender to the therapy site (coded as three levels: not accompanying, providing a ride only, participating in activities while there) was likewise unrelated to disposition, $\chi^2(4) = 7.23$, n.s. ($\tau = .04$). Phone contact between counselors and family members was somewhat related to disposition, $\chi^2(2) = 5.59$, $p = .06$ ($\tau = .02$).

Several other involvement variables showed strong positive relationships to outcome: Participating in the offender's homework assignments, $\chi^2(2) = 27.91$, $p < .001$ ($\tau = .16$); monitoring and reporting the offender's behavior to the therapist, $\chi^2(2) = 11.88$, $p = .002$ ($\tau = .07$); giving the therapist information about the offender's home situation and family history, $\chi^2(2) = 13.45$, $p = .001$ ($\tau = .08$); participating in individual or group therapy separate from the offender, $\chi^2(2) = 14.36$, $p < .001$ ($\tau = .08$); participating in family or couples counseling with the offender, $\chi^2(2) = 16.51$, $p < .001$ ($\tau = .09$); and signing a lifetime Relapse Prevention Plan, which outlines rules for the offender to live by, $\chi^2(2) = 34.89$, $p < .001$ ($\tau = .20$). In all cases, more family involvement was related to a greater likelihood of remaining in and completing treatment.

Several demographic variables were examined for their relationship to disposition. None of them was significant: For marital status (single, married, divorced), $\chi^2(4) = 5.21$ ($\tau = .03$); for education level (less than high school, high school degree, some college, college degree), $\chi^2(6) = 6.77$ ($\tau = .04$); for race/ethnicity (White, African-American, other), $\chi^2(4) = 3.68$ ($\tau = .02$); for age, $F(2,100) = 1.13$.

Interestingly, although marital status was not itself related to disposition, it was related to involvement. Family members of married offenders were more likely to be involved with treatment, $\chi^2(2) = 11.63$, $p = .003$ (τ for predicting involvement from marital status $= .11$); to call the therapist, $\chi^2(2) = 5.74$, $p = .06$ ($\tau = .05$); to monitor and report the offender's behavior, $\chi^2(2) = 5.72$, $p = .06$ ($\tau = .05$); to share details of the family situation and history, $\chi^2(2) = 8.99$, $p = .01$ ($\tau = .09$); and to participate in family or couples counseling, $\chi^2(2) = 5.55$, $p = .06$ ($\tau = .05$).

Recidivism

Only 7 (6.6%) of the men who participated in the program reoffended. All of these had left the program for some reason. None of the individuals who completed treatment or who were still in treatment reoffended.[2] Propensity to reoffend was unrelated to family involvement, $\chi^2(2) = 1.26$, n.s. ($\tau = .01$). Likewise, none of the other involvement variables was related to recidivism. Similarly, none of the demographic variables was related to recidivism.

Disposition was related to recidivism. For this analysis, only two levels of disposition were distinguished: left treatment and remained in treatment. Whether or not the individual remained in treatment was significantly related to propensity to reoffend, $\chi^2(1) = 5.32$, $p = .02$ ($\tau = .05$). Those who remained in treatment did not reoffend.

One note about the power of the chi-squared analyses is in order. The sample size of 106 insures adequate power to detect effects of moderate size in the data.[3] However, if the relationships among the variables are rather small, then a larger sample size would be needed.

For this reason, although one might be fairly confident of the significant results, the non-significant results should be viewed with caution.

DISCUSSION

This research examined several possible correlates of sexual offenders' decisions to remain in therapy. In particular, the research focused on the role of others' involvement in the success of therapy in a treatment program in North Carolina. One major outcome of the program so far is that the men whose families are involved stay in treatment. Table 1 shows that when the family is involved the offender is less likely to be dismissed from treatment for lack of progress; less likely to be removed or incarcerated; and less likely to withdraw voluntarily. When the family is involved, more than half of the offenders complete or are still in treatment. When the family is not involved, significantly fewer men–only 30 percent–remain in therapy.

Although previous research has suggested that marital status is related to treatment disposition (i.e., married men are more likely to remain in therapy, Hanson, Steffy, & Gautier, 1993), the present study did not replicate this finding. Instead, the results suggest that family involvement mediates any relationship that may exist between marital status and disposition. That is, the families of married men tend to involve themselves more in the treatment process than do the families of single or divorced men. It is this involvement itself that facilitates successful treatment. A future study with a larger sample could test this mediator model explicitly. Data supporting such a model would suggest that interventions aimed at increasing family participation would serve to bolster the success of sex offender treatment programs.

Recidivism rate was unrelated to any of the predictor variables examined here. These non-significant results could be due to the low incidence of recidivism and the small size of the present sample. The one clear finding emerging here links recidivism rate clearly to treatment disposition. Although we cannot infer causality from a correlational study, these findings simultaneously suggest the success of the treatment program and underscore the importance of reducing attrition.

Further study and follow-up is needed, over a longer period of time, to draw any definitive conclusions about the success of the current program. However, after tracking some of the men over a five-year period, indications are that the family systems approach reflects a margin of success in the treatment of adult male child molesters.

NOTES

1. For this initial analysis, even simple acts such as providing a ride to the client or talking to the therapist even to say that therapy was unnecessary, were counted as family involvement (calls to say the client would be absent from therapy were excluded, however). Such a definition, it was felt, would provide a conservative estimate of the impact of involvement on treatment outcome. If we focus only on more meaningful involvement, such as participation in support groups, providing information to the therapist, and involvement with the client's home assignments, the results are much more dramatic: $\chi^2(2) = 10.91$, $p = .004$.

2. More specifically, $\tau^{r/c}$ is an asymmetric measure describing the proportion of variation in the row variable R that can be predicted from membership in the column variable C. Goodman and Kruskal (1954) interpret $\tau^{r/c}$ as the relative decrease in the proportion of incorrect predictions about row membership (the criterion variable) when we utilize the information about column membership (the predictor variable); that is, when we base our predictions on conditional probabilities of row membership rather than on marginal probabilities. In all analyses involving treatment disposition, disposition is treated as the row (criterion) variable when computing $\tau^{r/c}$.

3. At first glance, one might logically conclude that the zero recidivism rate for those still in treatment is an artifact of the classification procedure for the disposition variable. That is, all people who reoffended would be reincarcerated and therefore would be classified as incarcerated. In fact, however, none of the men in the present study reoffended while still in treatment. For most men who were reincarcerated, the reason was other than a sexual offense. In one ambiguous case, a person reoffended just after being dismissed from the program and was incarcerated immediately for that offense. This person was classified as incarcerated, although he could just as easily have been placed in the "dismissed" category.

4. Effect size in the context of a chi-squared test of independence refers to the degree of relationship between the two variables in the analysis. In the case of 2 × 2 tables, the degree of relationship is easily measured using the Pearson product-moment correlation coefficient. In such circumstances, this correlation coefficient is called ϕ. Because it is a bonafide correlation, its square, ϕ^2 is correctly interpreted as the proportion of variability that the two variables share. A useful generalization of ϕ is provided by Cramér's ϕ statistic (Hays, 1994, p. 869):

$$\phi' = \sqrt{\frac{\chi^2}{N(r-1)}}$$

where χ^2 is the computed chi-squared statistic, N is the sample size, and r is lesser of the number of categories for the two variables. Strictly speaking, this generalization of ϕ does not share the same interpretations as in the case of the 2×2 table. However, one can roughly interpret the size of ϕ' in the same way.

With a sample size of 106, the power of the chi-squared tests used here to detect a moderate effect is equal to or greater than .80 at α level of .05, where moderate is defined as a population ϕ' of .30 (see Cohen, 1977, p. 204 ff). For comparison, the sample values of ϕ' for analyses of Tables 1 and 2 were on the order of .22. If we assume that the population effect is commensurate with this, that is $\phi' = .2$, then to obtain a power of .80 for all analyses (at α-level of .05), the sample size would have to be about 240. If the population effect in each case is as small as $\phi' = .1$, then a sample size of more than 800 would be necessary.

REFERENCES

Abbott, B.R. (1995). *Sexual reoffense rates among incest offenders eight years after leaving treatment.* San Jose, CA: Giarretto Institute.

Alexander, M. (1993, November). *Sex offender treatment: A response to the Furby et al., quasi-meta analysis.* Paper presented at the Association for the Treatment of Sexual Abusers 12th Annual Conference, Boston, MA.

Borduin, C.M., Henggeler, S.W., Blaske, and D.M., Stein, R. (1990). Multisystemic treatment of adolescent sexual offenders. *International Journal of Offender Therapy and Comparative Criminology, 35,* 105-114.

Cohen, J. (1977). *Statistical power analysis for the behavioral sciences* (2nd ed.). Hillsdale, NJ: Lawrence Erlbaum.

Goodman, L.A. & Kruskal, W.H. (1954). Measures of association for cross-classifications. *Journal of the American Statistical Association, 49,* 732-764.

Hanson, R.F., Lipovsky, J.A., Saunders, B.E. (1994). Characteristics of fathers in incest families. *Journal of Interpersonal Violence, 9(2),* 155-168.

Hanson, R., Steffy, R., Gauthier, R. (1993). Long-term recidivism of child molesters. *Journal of Consulting and Clinical Psychology, 61,* 642-652.

Hays, W.L. (1994). *Statistics* (5th ed.). New York: Harcourt Brace.

Henderson, J.E., English, D.J., and MacKenzie, W.R. (1989). Family centered casework practice with sexually aggressive children. *Journal of Child Sexual Abuse,* 89-110.

Henggeler, S.W. (1997). Treating serious antisocial behavior in youth: The MST approach. *Juvenile Justice Bulletin.* Washington, DC: U.S. Department of Justice, Office of Juvenile Justice and Delinquency Prevention.

Knopp, F.H. (1985). *Remedial intervention in adolescent sex offenses: Nine program descriptions.* Syracuse, NY: Safer Society Press.

Lockhart, L.L., Saunders, B.E., and Cleveland, P. (1989). Adult male sexual offenders: An overview of treatment techniques. *Journal of Child Sexual Abuse,* 1-32.

Marshall, W.L. and Pithers, W.D. (1994). A reconsideration of treatment outcomes with sex offenders. *Criminal Justice and Behavior, 21 (1),* 10-27.

Roesler, T.A., Savin, D., and Crosz, C. (1993). Family therapy of extrafamilial sexual abuse. Journal *of the American Academy of Child and Adolescent Psychiatry, 32* (50), 967-971.

Sieburg, E. (1985). *Family Communication.* New York: Gardner Press, Inc.

Silovsky, J.F., and Hembree-Kigin, T.L. (1994). Family and group treatment for sexually abused children: A review. *Journal of Child Sexual Abuse, 3*(3), 1-20.

Skynner, A.C.R. (1981). An open-systems, group-analytic approach to family therapy. *Handbook of Family Therapy,* 39-84. New York: Brunner/Mazel, Publishers.

Adult and Adolescent Female Sex Offenders: Experiences Compared to Other Female and Male Sex Offenders

L. C. Miccio-Fonseca, PhD

ABSTRACT. Female sex offenders ($N = 18$) were compared with male sex offenders ($N = 332$) and with females who were not sex offenders ($N = 215$) on various experiences in their personal histories. Female sex offenders who were victims of sexual abuse were compared to female sex offenders who were not. The present study is part of a comprehensive, seven-year research project described elsewhere (Miccio-Fonseca, 1995, 1996). The project dealt with comparative experiences and characteristics of adult and adolescent sex offenders, victims, and their families. The groups in the present study were analyzed with regard to an array of variables, including psychological, medical, gynecological, urological, drug, law enforcement, and homicidal and suicidal histories. Other variables studied were sexual difficulties and dysfunctions, sexual health, and life stressors.

Female and male sex offenders differed significantly on numerous psychological, life-stressor, and sexual variables. Female sex offenders differed significantly from females who were not sex offenders on the same sets of variables, and they were significantly younger. Implications for clinical practice with this population are discussed. *[Article*

L. C. Miccio-Fonseca, Psychologist and Researcher, is Clinic Director at the Clinic for the Sexualities in San Diego, California.

Address correspondence to L. C. Miccio-Fonseco, 591 Camino de la Reina, Suite 533, San Diego, CA 92108.

[Haworth co-indexing entry note]: "Adult and Adolescent Female Sex Offenders: Experiences Compared to Other Female and Male Sex Offenders." Miccio-Fonseca, L. C. Co-published simultaneously in *Journal of Psychology & Human Sexuality* (The Haworth Press, Inc.) Vol. 11, No. 3, 2000, pp. 75-88; and: *Sexual Offender Treatment: Biopsychosocial Perspectives* (ed: Eli Coleman, and Michael Miner) The Haworth Press, Inc., 2000, pp. 75-88. Single or multiple copies of this article are available for a fee from The Haworth Document Delivery Service [1-800-342-9678, 9:00 a.m. - 5:00 p.m. (EST). E-mail address: getinfo@haworthpressinc.com].

© 2000 by The Haworth Press, Inc. All rights reserved.

75

copies available for a fee from The Haworth Document Delivery Service: 1-800-342-9678. E-mail address: getinfo@haworthpressinc.com <Website: http://www.haworthpressinc.com>]

KEYWORDS. Sex offenders, female sex offenders, male sex offenders comparative experiences

In the last few years clinicians have seen a growing body of research literature regarding adolescent male sex offenders (e.g., Groth, 1977; Abel, G.G., Mittelman, M.S., & Becker, J. 1985; Fehrenbach, P.A., Smith, W., Monastersky, C., & Deisher, R. W. 1986; Becker, J.V., Kaplin, M.S., Cunningham-Rathner, J., & Kavoussi, R. 1986; Levin, S. M, & Stava, L. 1987; Miccio-Fonseca, 1994; Miccio-Fonseca, 1996; Cooper, Murphy, & Haynes 1996). The *Uniform Crime Reports* (1990) of the Federal Bureau of Investigation's compilation of monthly arrest statistics from law enforcement agencies throughout the United States, reported that of the sex crimes committed (excluding forcible rape and prostitution) 17% were committed by persons under the age of 18, with 10% under the age of 15. Males committed the vast majority of these sex crimes, accounting for about 95% of those reported. The U.S. Department of Justice, Office of Justice Programs, Bureau of Justice Statistics, (1997) found that the number of imprisoned rapists grew at a yearly average of about 7% over the fourteen years. Sex offenders accounted for about 1 in 5 violent offenders housed in state prisons in 1994. About 6 out of 10 sex offenders had been convicted of sexual assault, and 4 in 10 convicted of forcible rape. The largest category of sex offenders was composed of those serving time for molestation, fondling, or other related kinds of sexual assault. These figures primarily describe male sex offenders.

Compared to the research on male sex offenders, there have been few studies on female sex offenders (Davis & Leitenberg, 1987; Fehrenbach, & Monastersky, 1988; Kaplan and Green, 1995; Mathews, R. Hunter, J., & Vuz, J., 1997). The available research is almost all descriptive. The findings have indicated a heterogeneous group of individuals of all ages, cutting across all socioeconomic and racial backgrounds (Fehrenbach & Monastersky, 1988; Travin, Cullen, & Protter, 1990). Some researchers have focused on types of offenses and the ages and gender of victims (Fehrenbach & Monastersky, 1988; Travin, Cullen, & Protter, 1990; Mathews, Hunter, Jr., & Vuz, 1997). Kaplan and Green (1995) studied eleven female sex offenders, matched with an equal number of non-sex-offender females, all incarcerated. Travin et al. (1990) reviewed the existing literature on female sex offenders and concluded that there are a small number of these persons in the U.S. population. They also observed that much of the research focuses on sexually offensive behaviors in terms of type of offense, frequency, and types of victims. The literature offers little information on other dimensions, such as psychological histories, legal difficulties, life stressors, gynecological histories, sexual health, and violence in the family (Davis & Leitenberg, 1987; Fehrenbach & Monastersky, 1988; Scavo, 1989; Travin, Cullen, & Protter, 1990; Mathews, R., Hunter, Jr., & Vuz, 1997).

The present study attempts to fill this gap by exploring such variables as psychological histories, legal difficulties, life stressors, gynecological histories, sexual health, and violence in the family to determine whether they differentiate female sex offenders, female non-sex-offenders and male sex offenders. This study was a part of a comprehensive, seven-year research project described elsewhere (Miccio-Fonseca, 1996). The larger project compared experiences and characteristics of adult and adolescent sex offenders, victims, and their families.

METHOD

The subjects in this study were all from southern California and were either self-referred or referred by a law-enforcement official (probation officer, attorney, or judge) or by Child Protective Services. They were referred for a variety of purposes, such as psychotherapeutic treatment, consultation, or psychological evaluation. All subjects were interviewed for a minimum of 90-240 minutes. The subjects were part of a larger, ongoing research study that took place over a seven-year period. Female non-sex offenders came from families that included sexually abused victims or sex offenders.

A licensed psychologist interviewed individual subjects in a clinical setting. The psychologist specializes in the psychological sex disorder of Paraphilia Disorder, as defined in the *Diagnostic and Statistical Manual of Mental Disorders-IV.* Individual interviews lasted from ninety minutes to several hours. Each person completed an encyclopedic Female or Male Intake Questionnaire. These are multiple item questionnaires (for the Males there were 183 items, for the Females

194 items). These questionnaires are self-report instruments that cover a variety of areas with regard to the person's psychological, medical, urological, gynecological, drug, law enforcement, psychiatric illness, and homicidal and suicidal histories. Other items cover sexual health, sexual difficulties and sexual dysfunctions. In addition, both questionnaires include a number of items that are based on the Holmes-Rahe scale (Holmes & Rahe, 1967), asking respondents to check the life-stress events experienced during the preceding twelve months. The purpose of the assessment was to obtain a comprehensive picture of the person clinically, particularly with regard to sexuality. Since these data were collected as part of clinical practice and not specifically for a research study, informed consent was not necessary. There was no "treatment effect" being tested in this *post hoc* analysis of these clinical data.

Female sex offenders ($N = 18$, average age of 22) were compared with male sex offenders ($N = 332$, average age of 21) and with females who were not sex offenders ($N = 215$, average age of 34) on various experiences in their personal histories. Female sex offenders who were victims of sexual abuse were compared to those who were not. Although these N's are obviously uneven, the statistical comparisons were thought to be instructive, since the incidence of reported female sexual offense is so low in the general population.

In this study "sex offender" is defined as a person who either has admitted to, or been convicted of, a sex crime or has encountered legal difficulties such as allegations, arrests, convictions and/or custody because of his/her sexual habits other than prostitution. This definition covers such offenses as incest, rape, molestation, exhibitionism, and peeping. "Victim" is defined as a person who has reported experiencing sexual trauma, sexual abuse, (i.e., incest, rape, or molestation).

Subjects who could not read or were unable to complete the instruments were given one of the two forms of the questionnaire through structured interviews. Subjects who could complete the instruments on their own were also interviewed. Each questionnaire item was reviewed and explored with each subject further, and additional data were gathered in the process.

Statistical Analysis

Chi-square analyses were carried out on all categorical data, and one-way analyses of variance were computed for continuous variables. Both of these procedures "correct" for uneven *N*'s. Alpha was set at .05 for all tests of significance. In the following paragraphs all statistics reported represent statistically significant differences, and non-significant differences are not reported. The statistical inferences do not, of course, reflect the general population. The samples represent sub-populations of people who experience sexual trauma, who are sex offenders, or who are members of families that include sex offenders. No attempt was made to estimate the incidence of sex offense within the population of people in general, since the individuals and family samples were either self referred or referred by a law-enforcement official and because of the high probability that such offenses are underreported.

RESULTS

Subjects

Of the 18 female adolescent and adult sex offenders in this study, 13 were both offenders and victims, and 5 were offenders only.

Female Sex Offenders (N = 18) vs. Male Sex Offenders (N = 332). Demographics of the two groups indicate that 17% of the male sex offenders were married, and only 2 out of 18 female sex offenders were. Most of both groups were students–50% were female sex offenders and 72% were male sex offenders. Female and male sex offenders were found to be similar on the following variables: age, ethnic classification, educational level, job stress, or a number of stressful events experienced within the last year, or ever having had a legal problem.

Female Sex Offenders (N = 18) vs. Females Who Were Not (N = 215). These two groups were found to be similar on ethnic classification, occupation level, and job stress. Of the 18 female sex offenders, 2 (11%) were married, compared to 55% of the female non-sex offender. This could be an age effect, since the average age of the sex offenders was 22, while that of the non-sex-offenders was 34. Female sex offenders had an overall lower educational level. Of the 18 female sex offenders, 4 (22%) had at least some college, compared with 42% of the female non-sex offenders. This may also be an age effect.

Psychological Problems

Female Sex Offenders (N = 18) vs. Male Sex Offenders (N = 332). These two groups were not statistically significantly different on the degree of psychiatric problems in the family; having anyone in the family that had physically hurt or killed someone; or having experience in individual, couples, family, or group therapy. Also, female and male sex offenders were not statistically significantly different in their self-reported reasons for therapy, such as depression, relationship difficulty, anxiety, or sexual abuse. The two groups were not statistically significantly different with regard to psychotherapeutic treatment effectiveness. Of the female sex offenders 44% had tried suicide, compared with 15% of the males. Of the female sex offenders 50% came from families where someone had attempted suicide, compared to 8% of the males. The two groups were not statistically significantly different with regard to the individuals' method of suicidal attempts or family members' method of suicide and in the method that a family member used to hurt or kill someone else.

Female Sex Offenders (N = 18) vs. Females Who Were Not (N = 215). These two groups differed with regard to the extent to which they had engaged in individual and group therapy: While 83% of the female offenders reported having been in individual therapy, 53% of the female non-sex offenders had that experience. Only 14% of the female non-sex offender had been in group therapy, compared with 8 out of the 18 offenders. Female sex offenders and female non-sex offenders were found to be similar in their reasons for therapy such as depression, relationship difficulty, anxiety, and sexual abuse. These two groups were also found to be similar with regard to psychotherapeutic treatment effectiveness. On the question of suicide, female sex offenders and female non-sex offenders were found to be similar on the following variables: history of suicide in the family, method of family members' suicide, method of hurting someone physically, or killing some one. Suicide attempts were reported by 12% of the females who were not sex offenders, while 8 out of the 18 (44%) sex offenders had attempted suicide. These two groups differed on the experience of having a family member who physically hurt or killed someone; 10 out of 18 (56%) of the female offenders came from such a family, while only 27% of non-sex offenders reported this.

Life Stressors

Female Sex Offenders (N = 18) vs. Male Sex Offenders (N = 332). These two groups were found to be similar on a number of life-stressors. These include experiencing the death of a significant other, divorce or separation, illness of a family member or significant other, financial difficulties, arguments with significant others, change in boss, change in employer and change in residence. One statistically significant finding was that male sex offenders had more legal problems; 68% of the male sex offenders reported having various kinds of legal problems, compared with 63% of the female sex offenders.

Female Sex Offenders (N = 18) vs. Females Who Were Not (N = 215). There were several significant differences between female sex offenders and females with regard to life stressors, Table 1 summarizes these results. The groups were found to be similar on the following life-stressor items: death of a significant other, illness of a significant other, divorce, separation, personal lawsuit, financial difficulties, surgery, difficulties on the job, change in boss, change in employer, and change in residence.

Sexual Health and Sexual Histories

No subject in this study was known to be HIV-positive, and none reported being diagnosed with AIDS or ARC (AIDS-Related Symptom Complex).

Female Sex Offenders (N = 18) vs. Male Sex Offenders (N = 332). Male sex offenders reported having more sexual partners than females did; 43% of the male sex offenders reported having 2-5 sexual partners within the last year, compared with only 12% of the females. Of the female sex offenders, 44% reported having no sexual partner within the last year, compared with 11% of the males. Female sex offenders reported having a higher average number of sexual illnesses (Mean = 0.33) than male sex offenders (Mean = 0.08). The two groups were found to be similar with regard to sexual dysfunctions or sexual problems.

Female Sex Offenders (N = 18) vs. Females Who Were Not (N = 215). These two groups were found to be similar with regard to age of onset of menses, number of pregnancies, number of miscarriages, difficulties with pregnancy, and number of stillbirths. The finding regarding number of pregnancies and miscarriages are noteworthy, given the age disparity between the two groups. There were significant differences between these groups on the following gynecological-history variables: unwanted pregnancy, number of live births, and having had one or more abortions. Offender/victims had a higher average number of abortions (Mean = .89) than non-offenders (Mean = 0.27). Female sex offenders had fewer live births (Mean = 1.11) than female non-sex offenders (Mean = 2.38). Female non-sex offenders had a higher average number of surviving children (Mean = 2.37), than female sex offenders (Mean = 1.11). They also differed on the number of abortions; 6 out 18 (33%) of the female sex offenders had at least one abortion, compared with only 20% of the non-sex offenders. On sexual functioning and sexual health, female sex offenders and non-sex offenders were found to be similar on the following: lack of sexual desire, lack of sexual frequency, experiencing more frequency than desire; painful intercourse, lack of orgasm, and having no painful penetration. Additionally, the two groups were found to be similar on partner sexual problems, partners lack of relaxing and partners having performance anxiety. Regarding sexually transmitted diseases, the groups were found to be similar on the incidence of having genital herpes, anal herpes, chlamydia, Hepatitis B, and other sexual illness. Female sex offenders had reported a higher average number of sexual illnesses experienced in the past (Mean = .33) than non-offenders (Mean = .09).

TABLE 1. Significant Differences in Life Stressors Between Female Sex Offenders and Female Non-Sex Offenders.

Life Stressors	Female Sex Offenders N = 18	Female Non-Sex-Offenders N = 215
Trouble with the law	89%	52%
Trouble with the law due to sexual habit	44%	11%
Hospitalized	33%	13%
Problem with child(ren)	22%	64%
Relationship difficulty	50%	27%
Difficulty in school	33%	17%

Victims of Sexual Abuse

The percentage of victims of sexual abuse in this study was high; 50% of the male sex offenders reported having been sexually abused, compared to 72% of the female sex offenders and 52% of the female non-offenders. A higher proportion of female sex offenders, compared with either male sex offenders or female non-sex offenders, was sexually traumatized.

Female Sex Offenders (N = 18) vs. Male Sex Offenders (N = 332). Of the female sex offenders, 33% reported being a victim of incest, compared with 13% of the male sex offenders. Being a rape victim was reported by 39% of the female sex offenders, compared to 4% of the males. Female and male sex offenders were found to be similar with regard to being a victim of sexual molestation, assault, or sodomy.

Age when first traumatized was also different between the two groups. Of the female sex offenders, 54% were sexually abused by age six, compared to 33% of the male sex offenders. The two groups differed with regard to how they were sexually traumatized: 56% of the females reported having been penetrated, compared to 24% of the males. Of the females 67% had been fondled, compared to 39% of the males. Also, of the females 67% had been peeped at, compared to 34% of the males.

Female Sex Offenders (N = 18) vs. Females Who Were Not (N = 215). These two groups were found to be similar with regard to age when first sexually traumatized, as well as being victims of incest, assault, and sodomy. There were differences with regard to having been a victim of sexual molestation as a child: 10 out of 18 female sex offenders (56%), versus 32% of female non-sex offenders.

Sex Offenders and Their Victims

Male sex offenders differed with regard to their selection of victims; 15% of the male sex offenders reported having both male and female victims. Female sex offenders did not report having victims of both genders. Table 2 summaries the differences by type of victim.

DISCUSSION

In this study there was a small number of female sex offenders, compared to the number of male sex offenders and the number of

TABLE 2. Male and Female Sex Offenders by Type of Victim

Type of Victim	Female Sex Offenders N = 18	Male Sex Offenders N = 332
Female family member	20%	25%
Male family member	50%	4%
Female, whether in family or not	40%	64%
Male, whether in the family or not	60%	21%
Both females(s) and male(s)	0%	15%

female non-sex offenders. This pattern is similar to reports from U.S. Department of Justice, Office of Justice Programs, Bureau of Justice Statistics (1997), which found among sex offenders in state prisons for sexual assault, 1.2% were female. O'Connor (1987), who reviewed Home Office Criminal Statistics for the period 1975-84 in England and Wales; female offenders represented 0.95% of the total sex offenses reported. In the United States, Musk and Gallager (1985) found that 1.65% of the total female prison population surveyed were incarcerated for sexual offenses. Groth and Birnbaum (1979) found in a sample of 250 child molesters, female sex offenders represented only approximately 1% in incarcerated populations. On the other hand, these small numbers may reflect the under-reporting of female sexual offenses. For example, Risin and Koss (1987) found that 7.3% (N = 216) of 2972 male college students reported having been sexually abused before the age of 14. Of these male victims, 47% reported having been abused by females. Gray, Busconi, Houchens, and Pithers (1997) reported that in their sample of 72 children, 25% had been sexually abused by a female.

Although there was a small number of female sex offenders in the present study, there were numerous statistically significant differences. Even if the unequal group sizes cause concern about the validity of these differences, they are instructive. In other words, female sex offenders are probably describably different from male sex offenders and female-non-sex offenders. In the present study female sex offenders, female non-sex offenders, and male sex offenders are alike on a number of variables, but there are areas in which they are different. These findings suggest a need for further research.

One obvious limitation in this study is that the researcher conducted the clinical interviews. This practice of data gathering could have a contaminating effect. Further research could include alternative data-collection methods and more objective data gathering.

Another limitation of the study is self-reported sexual behavior and personal history. It is largely unknowable whether the 18 female sex offenders were completely forthcoming with regard to their own culpability. A majority (13 out of 18) claimed to have been victims of sexual abuse themselves. Such claims, of course, could be conscious or unconscious attempts by these females to minimize their responsibilities with regard to their own offenses. Their reports of suicide attempts may also have been, to some degree, a way of masking the personal culpability.

The rationale underneath the clinical-interview questionnaire was that the following general sets of variables could be meaningfully related to sexual offenses that involved victims, gynecological difficulties, sexual histories, psychological difficulties, family dysfunctions, extent of life stresses, violence against self and others, and legal difficulties. It was expected that female sex offenders would have backgrounds that would reflect negative status on such variables.

There were differences in a variety of areas of gynecological history between female offenders when compared with other females in this study. Such findings suggest that female sex offenders have a higher number of abortions. Also, they have more sexual illness than either male sex offenders or females that were non-sex offenders. The female sex offenders in this study were significantly younger than their counterparts who were no sex offenders. It is possible to conclude that these women were sexually irresponsible, promiscuous individuals. Alternatively, they may have simply become sexually active at an earlier age than did the non-sex-offenders. These findings suggest that gynecological check-ups and sex education need to be parts of treatment for such women. Further, the findings in the present study suggest that the overall poor sexual health and habits of the female sex offenders need attention. Education in family planning, parenting, addressing developmental issues in childhood, human sexuality, safer sex methods, and birth control should be included in the treatment regime of female sex offenders. Male offenders could benefit from similar educational treatment.

Sex offenders, whether male or female, tend to come from violent homes. Clinicians should also look for evidence of the battering syndrome with such patients. Clinicians should assess the lethality level of the individual, including but not limited to homicidal ideation, and determine whether a plan or methods of possible homicidal incidents are eminent. If there are indicators for further clinical actions, such as having to notify the possible intended victim or notifying authorities, the clinician should act immediately.

The data in this study also indicate that female sex offenders are more likely to attempt suicide or at least have a history of suicidal attempts. Clinicians should evaluate the extent to which such individuals are experiencing suicidal ideation. Clinicians need to assess the risk level regarding such patients, determining whether the individual has a plan and/or a method of possibly committing suicide. Active intervention may be necessary.

In this sample of male and female sex offenders, 80% of each gender were sexually abused by the age of ten. About one-third of the females and one-eighth of the males were victims of incest. Over half of these females had been sexually traumatized by age 6, compared with about one-third of the males. Whether the perpetrators of these sexual offenses were members of their victims' families or not, the acts invariably produce trauma within the family unit. Family therapy needs to be seriously considered as a part of treatment. Sex offenders tend to come from dysfunctional family systems. Working only with individuals and not the family system may undermine the success of individual therapy. Maybe the most appropriate locus of treatment is the family, even though not all of the offenders were incest victims. Educating and treating families as well as treating sex offenders can offer promise of breaking the cycle of sexual abuse.

At the individual level, the central task of therapy is the reduction of deviant erotic arousal for those individuals who are sex offenders. This may necessitate the use of such methods as relapse prevention, hormonal therapy, and decreasing deviant sexual fantasies. Some of these methods can be used in group settings as well as intensive individual treatment sessions.

Further research into the cognitive structures of female sex offenders is needed. A common view regarding male sex offender is that their crimes are less about sex and more about misguided retribution, power, and dominance. For the male sex offender, the view goes, feeling power and dominance is an important ingredient in sexually offending behavior. With respect to female sex offenders, there is an absence of a "common view"–or even an agreed-upon set of important ingredients-that could account for sexually offending behavior(s). The psychological histories explored in this study may be important building blocks to consider in exploring the cognition of female sex offenders.

REFERENCES

Abel, G., Mittelman, M.S., & Becker, J. (1985). Sexual offenders: Results of assessment and recommendations for treatment. In H. H. Ben-Aron, S. I. Hucker, & C.D. Webster (Eds.), *Clinical criminology* (pp. 191-205). Toronto, Ontario, Canada: MM Graphics.

Becker, J.V. Kaplin, M.S., Cunningham-Rathner, J., & Kavoussi, R. (1986). Characteristics of adolescent incest sexual perpetrators: Preliminary findings. *Journal of Family Violence, 1,* 85-97.

Cooper, C., Murphy W.D., & Haynes, M.R. (1996). Characteristics of abused and nonabused adolescent sexual offenders. *Sexual Abuse: A Journal of Research and Treatment, 8,* 2, 105-119.

Davis, G.L., & Leitenberg, H. (1987). Adolescent sex offenders. *Psychological Bulletin, 101* (3), 417-427.

Diagnostic and statistical manual of mental disorders. Fourth Edition. (1994). Washington, DC: American Psychiatric Association.

Deisher, R.W., Wenet, G.A., Paperny, D.M., Clark, T.F., & Fehrenbach, P.A. (1982). Adolescent sex offense behavior: The role of the physician. *Journal of Adolescent Health Care, 2,* 279-286.

Fehrenbach, P.A., & Monastersky, C. (1988). Characteristics of female adolescent sexual offenders. *American Journal of Orthopsychiatric, 58* (1).

Fehrenbach, P.A., Smith, W., Monastersky, C., & Deisher, R.W. (1986). Adolescent sexual offenders: Offender and offense characteristics. *American Journal of Orthopsychiatry 56,* 225-233.

Gray, A., Busconi, A., Houchens, P., and Pithers, W. (1997). Children with sexual behavior problems. *Sexual Abuse: A Journal of Research and Treatment, 9,* No.4, 267-290.

Greenfeld, L.A. (NCJ-163392, February 1997). *Sex offenses and offenders: An analysis of data on rape and sexual assault.* Washington, DC U.S. Department of Justice, Office of Justice Programs, Bureau of Justice Statistics.

Groth, N.A. (1977). The adolescent sexual offender and his prey. *International Journal of Offender Therapy and Comparative Criminology, 21,* 249-254.

Groth, N.A., & Birnbaum, H.J. (1978). Adult sexual orientation and attraction to underage persons. *Archives of Sexual Behavior, 7,* 175-181.

Groth, N.A., & Birnbaum, H.J. (1979). *Men who rape: The psychology of the offender.* Plenum Press: New York.

Holmes, P.H., & Rahe, R.H. (1967). The Social Readjustment Rating Scale. *Journal of Psychosomatic Research, 11,* 213-218.

Kaplan, M.S., & Green, A. (1995). Incarcerated female sexual offender: A comparison of sexual histories with eleven female nonsexual offenders. *Sexual Abuse: A Journal of Research and Treatment, 7, 4,* 287-300.

Levin, S. M, & Stava, L. (1987). Personality characteristics of sex offenders: A review. *Archives of Sexual Behavior, 16,* 57-59.

Mathews, R., Hunter, J. & Vuz, J. (1997). Juvenile female sexual offenders: Clinical characteristics and treatment Issues. *Sexual Abuse: A Journal of Research and Treatment, 9,* 3, 187-200.

Miccio-Fonseca, L.C., Jones, J.E. & Futterman, L.A. (1990). Sexual trauma and the premenstrual syndrome. *Journal of Sex Education & Therapy, 16,* 4, pp. 270-278.

Miccio-Fonseca, L.C. (1992). Sexual trauma: A factor in PMS severity. *Medical Aspects of Human Sexuality, 26,* 2, pp. 44.

Miccio-Fonseca, L.C. (1994). *Adolescent sex offenders.* San Diego: Clinic for the Sexualities.

Miccio-Fonseca, L.C. (1996). Comparative differences in psychological histories of sex offenders, victims and their families. *Journal of Offender Rehabilitation, 23,* Issue 3-4, 1996.

Miccio-Fonseca, L.C. (1997). *Personal Sentence-Completion Inventory.* Brandon, VT: Safer Society Press.

Musk, H. & Gallager, K. (1985). *Sexual and physical abuse among women inmates and their families: A national survey.* Lanham, Maryland: American Correctional Association.

O'Connor, A.A. (1987). Female sex offenders. *British Journal of Psychiatry, 150,* 615-620.

Scavo, Rebecca (1989). Female sex offenders: A neglected treatment group. *The Journal of Contemporary Social Work,* pp. 114-117.

Risin, L.I. & Koss, M.P. (1987). Sexual abuse of boys: Prevalence and descriptive characteristics of childhood victimizations. *Journal of Interpersonal Violence, 2,* 3, 390-919.

Uniform Crime Report (1990). Washington, DC: Federal Bureau of Investigation.

Travin, S., Cullen, K., & Protter, B. (1990). Female sex offenders: Severe victims and victimizers. *Journal of Forensic Sciences, 35,* 140-150.

RESPECT ™:
A 7 Step System to Treat Pedophiles Who Are Mentally Retarded, Have Mental Illness, and Physical Handicaps

Thomas P. Keating, MA, LCSW, RT

SUMMARY. The RESPECT[TM] System is a 7 step program using a group setting to modify behavior and thinking patterns of pedophiles who are mentally retarded, have mental illness and physical handicaps. The System addresses issues of resistance, denial, empathy for the victim, self-esteem, plan development, and plan evaluation, by the entire group. Due to learning experiences many of the members have had in institutions and other environments at early stages of their development, the RESPECT[TM] program is one of habilitation. A perpetrator learns a graduated system of choices that empowers him to trust himself in his community. At the present time there are 14 pedophiles attending the group. Five have been adjudicated. Nine are in some type of supervised living program i.e., State Hospital, four live on their own; one is married. Other secondary diagnostic descriptions are Personality Disorder, Paranoid Personality Disorder, Schizophrenia, Paranoid Type, Schizophrenia, Disorganized Type, Alcohol Dependence, Impulse Control Disorder, ADHD, and Dysthymic Disorder. Also explored are cer-

Thomas P. Keating is Clinician, Psychiatric Day Treatment, BUDD, Program, Lipton Center, Fitchburg, MA 01420.

More information on the RESPECT [TM] system can be obtained on the World Wide Web at <http://www.ummed.edu/pub/k/kfletche/kidsurv.htm>.

[Haworth co-indexing entry note]: "RESPECT[TM]: A 7 Step System to Treat Pedophiles Who Are Mentally Retarded, Have Mental Illness, and Physical Handicaps." Keating, Thomas P. Co-published simultaneously in *Journal of Psychology & Human Sexuality* (The Haworth Press, Inc.) Vol. 11, No. 3, 2000, pp. 89-114; and: *Sexual Offender Treatment: Biopsychosocial Perspectives* (ed: Eli Coleman, and Michael Miner) The Haworth Press, Inc., 2000, pp. 89-114. Single or multiple copies of this article are available for a fee from The Haworth Document Delivery Service [1-800-342-9678, 9:00 a.m. - 5:00 p.m. (EST). E-mail address: getinfo@haworthpressinc.com].

© 2000 by The Haworth Press, Inc. All rights reserved.

tain counterresistence issues experienced by the writer and their resolution. *[Article copies available for a fee from The Haworth Document Delivery Service: 1-800-342-9678. E-mail address: getinfo@haworthpressinc.com <Website: http://www.haworthpressinc.com>]*

KEYWORDS. Sex offenders, pedophiles, mental retardation, mental illness, treatment

INTRODUCTION

Many dually diagnosed individuals (pedophiles) in sex offender treatment have not learned the basics of community living and have actually learned sexually aberrant behaviors while in the institutions that were responsible for their welfare. Therefore, the RESPECT™ System is one of habilitation. Wettstein, (1998) reports:

> Due to developmental impairments, the offender with mental retardation likely has never attained an adequate level of personal and societal independence A disproportionate percentage of defendants with mental retardation are poor, living at the margin, and powerless (McGee and Menolascino, 1992). The goal of habilitation becomes an educative or skill development one to ensure that the person acquires those personal-social and community-survival skills needed to ensure social independence and encourage respect for the code of conduct expected by the community. (p. 357)

The RESPECT™ system attempts to enhance personal accountability by including the following characteristics described by Wettstein (1998):

1. Teach or strengthens specific alternatives to offending behavior when confronted with conditions similar to those in which the behaviors previously occurred. Then develop more general problem-solving and coping skills. (Goldstein & Glick, 1987)
2. Teach/strengthen internalized standards against which the person can judge contemplated behaviors and which will provide the personal motivation to avoid unacceptable ways of acting. Including teaching/strengthening and internalizing rules that gov-

ern the person's social behaviors (Hayes, 1989). This can be accomplished in a program that (a) has clearly defined and understood rules of social living, (b) places responsibility on the person for respecting the rules, (c) systematically models and labels rule compliance and routinely reinforces it with valued consequences, and (d) routinely and promptly consequates rule-breaking. (pp. 358-359)

It is also suggested that the initial phase of treatment should be in a secure environment. Many of the sex offenders in the RESPECT™ treatment system are in residential settings that are not secure.

The RESPECT™ treatment system is concrete, repetitive, and activates at least seven intelligences described by Gardner (1983): linguistic, logical/mathematical, intrapersonal, spatial, musical, bodily/kinesthetic, and interpersonal. The system integrates all of these learning possibilities and activates behavior using one word cues. Cognitive restructuring is highly effective with this high-risk population, in limited trials, when learning is adapted to their individual learning problems and resources Haaven, Little, and Miller (1990):

> Linking emotion to the learning process. Residents retain what they are taught if the learning experience is fun, dramatic, or bizarre.

> Teaching is keyed to the resident's multiple intelligences. . . Teaches concepts and skills using art, music, role-playing, and other creative nontraditional activities. (p. 22)

Wettstein (1998):

> The cognitive and motivational-emotional characteristics of the offender with mental retardation frequently have not developed sufficiently to effectively assimilate the lasting effects of incarceration. Again, the internalization of standards of societal conduct and the related cognitive-motivational skills to use these under future conditions will best be accomplished in a program environment that is designed specifically to teach these and related skills of personal or self-management. (Gardner & Cole, 1989; Liberman, DeRisi, & Mueser, 1989) (p. 359)

The RESPECT™ System involves seven steps, which are mastered in sequence by group members, according to their own rate of progress, but with support and participation of the entire group. Groups vary in size from nine to fourteen members. Some members attend weekly, some attend only once a month, depending on their rate of progress and their learned ability to return safely to their communities. Several group members are remanded to the group for the period of their probation.

In summary Wettstein (1998) notes:

> Treatment programs should address the constellation of individually specific personal features and community-survival skills deficits. To accomplish meaningful therapeutic results, the treatment program should be diagnostically based, reflect a competency enhancement (habilitation) focus, and place major emphasis on teaching personal responsibility for one's actions. (p. 359)

Murphy, Coleman, and Haynes, (1983) note:

> While experienced clinicians who work with both disabled and non disabled sex offenders recognize more similarities than differences between the two populations, there is an appalling lack of research, studies and treatment models in the literature to assist in treatment planning for intellectually disabled sex offenders compared to the treatment resources available for non disabled sex offenders. (pp. 22-23)

Treatment information and resources become even more scarce when individuals are also carrying a Mental Illness diagnosis, and Physical Handicaps. Another challenge was to develop a model in an outpatient setting where the group meets only once weekly for one and one-half hours, and the client returns to his respective community. Although the habilitation model of the mental retardation service delivery system holds more promise of success than either punishment or illness models of the criminal justice and mental health systems (Wettstein, 1998), the typical habilitation programs are not sufficiently specialized and diverse to address the specific needs of the offender with mental retardation (Laski, 1992).

In summary, the usual programs offered by the criminal justice, mental health, and mental retardation systems seldom are satisfactory in meeting the special habilitation needs of the offender with mental retardation (Wettstein, 1998).

The critical starting point in the habilitation process is that the offender is accountable and responsible for his actions. The offender with mental retardation too frequently is not held accountable for his/her behavior by family and friends. This practice labeled as *psychological welfarism* by Gardner (1991) tends to reinforce the attitude that criminal behavior will be tolerated and overlooked. The result of this practice is repeated criminal behavior (Wettstein, 1998).

Internal control may also be lacking in the intellectually disabled individual with a mental illness and characterized by a greater degree of impulsivity than a non disabled offender. He may have a highly externalized "locus of control" perceiving many of the controlling factors in life as being "out there." As a result, he may feel frustrated and disempowered, unable to control what is happening to him; if he is in residential care, this perception may have been fostered by those very institutions. He is also more likely to use instrumental violence due to a lack of verbal skills, low tolerance for frustration and a tendency to panic in new situations.

Words and phrases often repeated and mimicked, by the disabled individual, can be confusing and contradictory.

> Example: A client's face, flushed grim; hands balled into fists, in a loud, threatening, voice, says, "I love you! I love you!"

The concept/thought of RESPECT™ connects specific body movements to concrete actions. The action is a martial arts bow taught to me by a client who is deaf, mildly mentally retarded, and schizophrenic, who took nine years to earn his Black Belt in Tai Kwon Do Karate. It is a combination of 7 distinct body movements ending with verbal and American sign language, "Respect Community." This is an example of respecting and using the client's frame of reference; creating an action where thoughts are congruent and concretely connected to body movement. The Bow takes 7 seconds to perform and is called, by the offender group, the RESPECT™ Bow. Each group begins and ends with RESPECT™.

D.M. Cull, Forensic Psychologist, Australia, (personal communication, September, 2, 1997) response to RESPECT™ (*Forum*, 1997):

> A baby is born with dignity. It presumes its needs will be met. It has a birthright to be loved, protected, guided supported and instilled with a sense of integrity. The dignity with which that

child is born is very frequently eroded through life's events. Some such individuals go on to become sex offenders. A few years ago I was informed, by a sex offender nonetheless, of the actual definition of the word *rehabilitation*. To quote this man–whose mental faculties are certainly not impaired, whose attitude in defining this word was well intended and respectful, "Rehabilitation is to reinvest with dignity." Whilst confrontation and direct challenge is frequently necessary to break through the barrier of defensive resistance to change, the process I believe most importantly must serve to recognize the damaged ego and serve to *reinvest* rather than to *further damage* the dignity of the person with whom the work is being done.

Regardless of whether the client is a pedophile, rapist, exhibitionist or any other offender of similar ilk, I invite the therapist to explore the issues which may well have ('I believe will have') underpinned or seriously damaged the dignity with which the client is born.

. . . I am even more appreciative, in fact indebted, to my client, B. . . , wherever he may now be, for teaching me the simplest yet most important piece of learning which all my formal training somehow forgot to impart. He came to me for learning and in the process gave to me the greatest piece of learning of my career.

Finally, the lesson to be learnt from this realization, I believe, is that we lose ourselves in all of all the theory and doctrine which is available, and essential, within this professionally precise field of endeavor, and overlook this simple yet vital aspect of our work within the field of rehabilitation of sex offenders. May our own presumably intact egos not be so inflated that we close our eyes and our ears to the opportunity to learn from the true experts in the field–our client group. I will remember that to *rehabilitate* is to *reinvest with dignity*.

The central concept of the RESPECT[TM] System is habilitative, i.e., to start from the beginning; *invest with dignity.* If an offender reoffends after completing the RESPECT[TM] System, and returns to the group, we *reinvest with dignity.* The process now is rehabilitative and he begins the entire process again.

Psychological treatments work best when they provide not specific remedies for particular problems but *tools* for managing any situation that might arise (Bandura, 1997). Treatment should equip people to take control of their lives and start a process of self-regulative change guided by a resilient sense of personal efficacy.

The RESPECT™ System is referred to by the therapist and participants as a *tool* to use over and over again when challenging thoughts, impulses, and behaviors surface. When an individual completes the entire program and has completed Step 7, the TRUST step, he has solved only one problem/reality. The first time through the entire system is only an introduction to the RESPECT tool. Everyone in the group knows that pedophilia is forever and there is no cure. If a new reality/problem presents itself, the offender will begin with Step 1, REALITY, to solve the new problem, but keep Step 7, TRUST. If he reoffends, he loses Step 7, TRUST. Once an offender has earned TRUST he struggles to keep it by using his program and not reoffending. The offender has learned positive CHOICES, Step 6, that he has built from his own frames of reference, in his own words. He has seen, said, heard, and acted on his commitment to himself. He hopefully has internalized the principles and the process. Through habilitation and rehabilitation he has invested and reinvested in his own dignity. The goal is to put RESPECT between thoughts that challenge community safety and an individual's behavior.

A quote by the German poet/philosopher, Goethe is the theme that runs throughout the entire program: If you treat an individual as he is, he will stay as he is. But, if you treat him as if he were what he ought to be and could be, he will become what he ought to be and could be.

THE R-E-S-P-E-C-T SYSTEM

The following are four cornerstone principles of the RESPECT™ treatment system:

Solution Focused

Dejong and Berg (1998) note:

> . . . the helping professions in the past have largely committed themselves to working with their clients through the application

of scientific expertise–accumulated scientific knowledge about problems and solutions. One consequence of this is that, wittingly or unwittingly, the helping professions have encouraged practitioners to believe and act as though their perceptions about their clients' problems and solutions are more important to the helping process than are the client's perceptions. In fact, the professional literature teaches that clients' perceptions often get in the way of professional practice because they are the source of client resistance, which practitioners work hard to overcome. (p. 19)

The clients' words and frames of reference are used to describe the individual steps and the group has to agree on the words used.

In solution building we insist that clients are the experts about their own lives.

. . . we do not view ourselves as expert at scientifically assessing client problems and then intervening; instead, we strive to be expert at exploring clients' frames of reference and identifying those perceptions that clients can use to create more satisfying lives. (p. 20)

It has also been my experience that an individual with mental retardation and a mental illness communicates much differently than I, as a professional clinician. *Their* words reflect their thinking process which is quite different from my own. If an offender's words are used, it will be his beginning of owning the problem and working toward his individualized solution.

Rituals

The RESPECT™ Bow is a ritual that is practiced at the beginning, during, and end of each group meeting. Rituals give individuals and families/groups possibilities to be the makers and interpreters of their lives (Black and Roberts, 1998). Consider the action of genuflecting and making the sign of the cross when Catholics enter their church; martial artists bowing to their Sifu (teacher) in respect of his wisdom; a wedding toast, a funeral eulogy. These action symbols embrace complicated concepts, with short, simple and repetitive movements and words. Symbols embrace meaning that cannot be easily expressed in words (Black and Roberts, 1998). Symbols and symbolic actions are powerful activators of sensory memory-smells, textures, and sounds (Black, Roberts, 1998). During the SELF-ESTEEM, Step 3, as many physical senses as possible are activated: scented candles are lit; classical music played; fruit, ice cream, cake, eaten; and a multi-colored floral arrangement is displayed. This self-esteem ritual is seen, said, heard, smelled, touched and tasted. It is a place of transition from problem focus to solution building. Because of their action and sensory elements, rituals appeal to all ages (Black and Roberts, 1998). All sex offenders in the RESPECT^{TM} System are developmentally delayed and have mental, intellectual, and emotional maturation ranging from 5 to 16 years of age. Rituals can help create meaning of where our lives have been and where they are going. A wedding signals a transition from aloneness. A funeral honors the transition from the physical to spiritual. Both are rituals with specific movements and actions with a specific purpose that transcends the words/language used. Rituals also embrace both constancy and transformation (Black and Roberts, 1998). Through rituals, repetitive actions, and celebration, RESPECT^{TM} becomes a true-north principle that is constant and gives the offender direction through difficult changes and transformation.

Accelerated, Multi-Sensory Learning Techniques

On average, we remember 20% of what is read, 30% hear, 40% see, 50% say, 60% do, and 90% of what we see, hear, say, and do (Rose, 1992). We also have multiple intelligences, which include bodily/physical, mathematical/logical, visual/spatial, inter-personal, intra-personal, linguistic, musical–none of which is fixed (Gardner, 1985). Although some people have very strong learning preferences, "multisensory" provides the best chance for successful, long-lasting learning for the majority. Multisensory learners deliberately engage all their senses as they learn. Since we appear to have a separate memory for what we see, what we hear, and what we do, the deliberate combination of all our senses makes for highly efficient learning. So V.A.P. it. Visual. Auditory. Physical (p. 45).

Example: The RESPECT^{TM} BOW takes 7 seconds to perform. The offender sees the bow (visual); hears the words, "Ko day, Kodah, Kodee (deaf client's words/frame of reference) Thank you, Respect your community" (auditory), and imitates the physical movements performed by the leader doing the bow (physical). When the leader finishes doing the RESPECT^{TM} Bow with each individual group member, (repetition) he will stand in the center of the group and receive RESPECT^{TM}, simultaneously, by the entire group. This exercise is also effective in breaking down an individual's isolation.

Everyone who comes into the group gets a RESPECT^{TM} card. On this card, phone numbers and addresses of other group members, can be written. This is also a concrete way to break down feelings of isolation and gives a perpetrator the beginnings of a respectful identification. The letters on the card are raised; you can feel, see, and touch RESPECT(TM). A laminated RESPECT^{TM} card is also offered which a perpetrator can pay $7.00. When he completes the first step he gets $1.00 back; by the time he has completed the seventh step, TRUST, he has earned back his $7.00 and has concretely invested in his future.

Self-Efficacy

Wylie, M. (1998) notes:

> Offenders live in a society that ostensibly considers them the scum of the earth, and many of them–if they think about it–are inclined to agree, which is why they become such pros at *not* thinking about it, by denying their own actions and blaming the victim. Denial, in all its guises, is less painful, then looking at the truth. In a sense, they have bought the common argument that the offender *is* the offense, so to admit the latter is to admit to their own irredeemable depravity There is no way out of this position; either lie and deny, and salvage some remnant of personal worth– not to mention avoid jail–or tell the truth and be damned. (p. 56)

Wettstein et al. found that the inherent life experience of the MR, MH, Pedophile has been one of living with these realities. A number of writers describe these sociopsychological features as including broken homes, improper physical conditions, low moral and ethical standards, unwholesome personal and interpersonal relationships, and a high percentage of parents and siblings presenting mental retardation and psychiatric difficulties.

Bandura, A. (1997) notes:

> *Motivational*: People motivate themselves by forming beliefs about what they can do, anticipating likely outcomes, setting

goals, and planning courses of action. Their motivation will be stronger if they believe they can attain their goals and adjust them based on their progress. Self-efficacy beliefs, the goals people set for themselves, how much effort they expend, how long they persevere, and how resilient they are in the face of failure and setbacks.

Mood or Affect: How much stress or depression people experience in threatening or difficult situations depends largely on how well they think they can cope. Efficacy beliefs regulate emotional states in several ways: (1) People who believe they can manage threats are less distressed by them; those who lack self-efficacy are more likely to magnify risks. (2) People with high self-efficacy lower their stress and anxiety by acting in ways that make the environment less threatening. (3) People with high coping capacities have better control over disturbing thoughts. Research shows that what causes distress is not the sheer frequency of the thoughts but the inability to turn them off. People with high self-efficacy are able to relax, divert their attention, calm themselves, and see support from friends, family and others. (p. 4)

The combination and interaction of these four principles: (1) Solution Focus. (2) Rituals. (3) Multi-sensory learning techniques and (4) Self-Efficacy create a strong internal desire to be trusted. Once TRUST is reached, it replaces the propensity to offend.

SEVEN STEPS TO TRUST

The steps are drawn on white poster board, are multicolored (visual) and placed on an alter/table (beginning of respect ritual) as a center-piece for the group. Each step is in a *client's words* (frame of reference). **R** is Reality: You have got to own it to change it . . **E** is Empathy: Knowing what the other person is going through and being there. **S** is Self-Esteem: Before you can do anything, you have to love yourself. You'll do more harm if you don't love yourself; then you can do anything and think halfway decent. **P** is Plan: The problem is like a puzzle. You have to have the right pieces to put it together. If you don't have the last piece it's not complete. **E** is Evaluation: we call this step simply, evaluation. **C** is Choice: This group gives me confidence so I can make a choice. **T** is Trust: Those steps are no malarkey. This group works. Look at me. I'm on the TRUST Step. I can go out into the community. I only have to come every other week. If I see a kid, I just walk away. The combination of the individual steps spell out the acronym RESPECT^{TM}. The group and I agree that the act of respecting ourselves and all others is a beginning and integral part of the solution to the problem of pedophilia.

When an individual first enters the sex offender group he will be asked if he wants to participate in the RESPECT^{TM} Bow. He may agree or refuse. If he agrees he is literally applauded by the entire group. If a group member originally refuses to do the respect bow, his decision is accepted, and he is given the RESPECT^{TM} Bow, regardless. If he chooses, sometime in the future to participate, the entire group applauds his action/participation. The message is clear and repetitious: respect, for oneself and all others, is unconditional. The Bow's intent is transferable to other situations outside of the group. A comment I often hear is:

> I saw the kid, she was looking at me and I remembered the bow (ritual). I walked away. I showed the kid respect.

This is a multi-sensory activity and one of the group's respect rituals.

Leadership

The therapist asks, "Who wants to be the leader today?" An individual who, throughout his entire lifetime has always been chosen last or not at all, will now have a chance at recognition. Another group dynamic is some of the individuals have histrionic and narcissistic personality disorders, and will struggle to be the center of attention in negative ways. The offer of leadership channels these attention-getting behaviors into positive actions. Newman, Scheuermann, Stephens, Dyer observed "Abraham Maslow addressed human personality in terms of a hierarchy of needs. According to him, man had the following needs in this order: food, water, safety, security, belongingness, love, and self-actualization. Thus personality develops around a capacity and drive to meet these needs" (1991, Feb. 22). Individuals who are MR, MH usually have the first four of these seven needs met by provider agencies, thus leaving energy to focus on the last three needs of Maslow's hierarchy. Belongingness, love, and self-actualization has, more often than not, been denied individuals attending the RESPECT^{TM} group.

The client who wants the leadership position has to stand up and say, "I do. My name is . . . I am a pedophile. This is my offense. I . . ." He "owns" his reality in as much detail as he is ready to give. The therapist can ask specific questions about his offense. The perpetrator can choose or not choose to elaborate. The perpetrator then proceeds to give each group member the RESPECT^{TM} Bow. Participation and initiating the bow makes the person vulnerable in a safe place and in a safe way. Allowing yourself to be vulnerable, if only for a moment, develops the beginnings of trust. Eye contact is important. The leader bows to each man in the group and each man can choose or not choose (empowerment) to participate. When the leader finishes giving each individual the RESPECT^{TM} Bow, he stands erect, in the center of the room. The entire group then gives him the RESPECT^{TM} Bow. There are usually 2 to 3 volunteers weekly who want to be leaders.

Leaders, after they explain their offense, have to agree to speak last. Many of the men have borderline, narcissistic, and histrionic types of disorders and want to be center of attention. Agreeing to speak last addresses this problem with the least amount of control by the therapist, and teaches patience.

STEP 1. REALITY: *You Have Got to Own It to Change It*

Since most perpetrators minimize their offenses, are in denial, even in the face of unequivocal evidence to the contrary, the members of the group cannot use words that minimize, evade or shift blame to their victims.

Wettstein (1998) notes:

> Perhaps the most important issue to be addressed in assessment is denial and minimization. Denial and minimization are often the result of the offender lying, but they are also the result of a psychological process involving distortion, mistaken attribution, rationalization, and selection attention and memory. The process serves to reduce the offender's experience of blame and responsibility for his offenses, and it seems to be successful. (p. 293)

The deep desire to be noticed and recognized as someone of worth, and a possible chance to be a step above the other members, can often crack denial of the offense. Some men have just come into the group and are on the REALITY^{TM} Step. Other group members, who have been in the group longer, are on higher steps, and have owned their realities, will often volunteer to lead. They have had positive experiences owning their problem and are not afraid to talk about their offenses. They are also esteemed members-leaders. The offender, who has been in denial for weeks or even months, will, at some time, want to be leader, because of the need to be self-actualized. There is indeed a powerful struggle that builds over the weeks as he sees how leaders are treated by the group. In ten years I have experienced only one person that wouldn't own his problem. He is now incarcerated.

The therapist uses the perpetrator's words to explain any of the steps so the offender can develop a sense of his own worth, ownership of his problem, in *his* words, and an understanding that it is something he gives to his own therapy. To threaten or coerce is counter-productive to treatment goals and is redundant. It has been my experience that these two interventions have been used unsuccessfully throughout his life. Haaven et al. found intellectually disabled offenders respond to teaching that is concrete, repetitive, and respects their humanity.

As much choice as possible should be left up to the client. He needs to know and to practice control of his own life. When he eventually gets to the TRUST step he will have had the opportunity to practice the skills he will need in his community to make the right decisions. In the RESPECT^{TM} System, the opportunity to be group leader creates the cognitive dissonance and internal confrontation the perpetrator needs to experience to break down the denial of his problem.

STEP 2. EMPATHY: *Understanding What the Other Person Is Going Through and Being There*

Campbell, (1989) notes:

> Although communication and empathy are related, empathy is not primarily aimed at exchanging information or altering another's belief or action systems. On the contrary, empathy is concerned rather with aligning one's state of mind with another's in order to commune rather than communicate, and in order to expand the interactive repertoire between the participants rather

than transmit knowledge. Empathy is putting oneself into the psychological frame of reference of another, so that the other person's thinking, feeling and acting are understood, and to some extent predictable. (p. 247)

Among group members, empathy involves entering the reality of the child the offender has abused. During this step we explore sexual abuse in the context of the victim. One group member compared his fear of going to the dentist to that of a child's fear during sexual abuse. The group also introduces role play during this step. Sometimes, the therapist can stand on a chair, over the perpetrator, and use the words/ language used during an offense, as the perpetrator, who remains seated, looks up at his own behavior. The sexual abuse experience that the client has suffered will frequently surface. Films like, *Why God? Why Me?* (Varied Directions) are also introduced and discussed.

The concept of empathy is exceedingly difficult for MR, MH, pedophiles to grasp and understand. Many can spend an entire year on this step alone. To finally think of another person, outside of the self, in an organized manner, someone that has been victimized by the client's behavior, is extraordinarily ego-dystonic.

I stood in her feet. I saw me. I did not like it.

The group's commonalty with the same problem, working toward the same solution, and literally seeing others succeed at owning their problems, without retribution and fear, and the desire to belong, allows the courage to risk a look at what one has done to another.

A man spends 2 and 1/2 years in prison for sexually molesting his 7 year old granddaughter; has been in the group 2 years, and is still on the REALITY Step. He is describing a flashback experience of his own sexual abuse by an uncle.

... and he did it to me for a long time. Years. Oh! Oh my God! I did to her (granddaughter) what he did to me.

This man moved on to the SELF-ESTEEM Step # 3 and identified that step for the rest of the group.

STEP 3. SELF-ESTEEM: Before You Can Do Anything, You Have to Love Yourself. You'll Do More Harm to People if You Don't Love Yourself. Then, You Can Do Anything and Think Halfway Decent

A client asks, "Am I dirty?"

This is a celebration step, marking the courage of a member who has taken the previous two steps, and building on the client's strengths to move on to recovery. This step also activates and stimulates as many senses as possible and the seven intelligences of accelerated learning techniques. The seven intelligences involve multistimuli (Rose, 1995). In the group space, we celebrate the individual who has completed Step 2. Empathy. This is his day, his celebration. Scented candles are lit; flowers, fruit, delicious food is brought in and classical music is played. Surrounded by soothing sounds and colors, we make an individual's progress memorable (ritual). Isolation is broken down for appropriate reasons. Clients who are on earlier steps are motivated to move up to the next level.

Black and Roberts (1998) describe Family Traditions: The Inside Calendar:

> In family traditions, day to day activity is altered to celebrate special dates such as the formation of the family (anniversary), entrance into the world (birthday), family connections (reunions, or distinct family times (like vacations). They are on what we call the *inside calendar* of the family. (p. 16)

The Self-Esteem celebration is only known to the group and is for group members only. This act of celebrating together offers an opportunity for an isolated individual to connect with others with a common problem. The MR, MH, pedophile almost always acts alone when committing his offense. He is now in the company of others who have owned their problem, empathized with their victims and survived. Those on the higher steps pass down their knowledge and the beginner begins to see the possibility and value of change in a concrete way. He begins to share feelings, fears, crimes, and hopes that he will not share outside of the group. He feels safe. The group, for some offenders, becomes family. "This group is like family to me. I say stuff here I can't say anywhere else."

A client asks, "Am I dirty?"

Another client responds: No. You are not dirty. You have a problem, like the rest of us.

This step also leads to significant achievement motivation. Group members who are still in denial start to experience considerable inner turmoil. According to Glasser (1975), people strive constantly to fulfill their needs, and when they are unsuccessful, they begin to behave unrealistically. During this step we begin to explore the first time a pedophile started feeling guilt when a supposedly positive experience was happening.

At this juncture in the treatment System, the group tends to become cohesive and gain its own momentum as members assimilate and exchange information, often unconsciously. It is during this step that the group begins to explore the concept of forgiveness. This is not absolution but an exploration about healing what was usually thought of as unforgivable and hopeless.

Rituals help us recognize who we are and what we value and to come together in community to share and acknowledge both the joy and pain of our existence (Black and Roberts, 1998).

STEP 4. PLAN: The Problem Is Like a Puzzle. You Have to Have the Right Pieces to Put It Together. If You Don't Have the Last Piece, It's Not Complete

Some pedophiles state that they experience thought insertion or thought pressure, which results in clients assuming little or no responsibility for their sexual fantasies or other mental processes. This is particularly true of schizophrenic clients. In these diagnostic groups no external pressure is alleged: rather the patients assert that the irresistible force arises within their own minds, Campbell (1989). Also known as *pressure of ideas*.

The Plan step of the RESPECT™ System requires that pedophiles develop a behavioral plan that begins at the first thought of a child. Each client, to progress through the Plan step must start to write down their plan in a notebook that is provided. A RESPECT™ card, unlaminated, is usually placed on the cover. After writing the plan in their notebook, a time is picked to present their plan to the entire group for approval. This plan is written on a blackboard. If the client cannot write, the therapist will write for the client.

A typical Plan, developed by a hospitalized client from a locked ward in an area mental institution (incarcerated for multiple offenses in Oregon and Massachusetts) wrote down his plan as follows:

A. **R**eality
   Empathy
   Self-Esteem
   Plan
   Evaluation
   Choice
   Trust
B. Problem
   How can it be solved.
   How can you prevent it from happening again
C. The problem is like a puzzle–unless you have all the pieces it can't be fixed.
   a. thought
   b. erection
   c. child
   d. trouble
   e. memories
   f. relapse

D. Plan

Problem: Pedophilia and going after little children at the ages of 10 and under which was a denial at first but then after a few months of counseling I've come to realize that what I had done was wrong, and that something must be done.

How can it be fixed? After going to counseling I have come to develop a plan which will be mentioned in the next section.

How can I prevent it from happening again? I have come to develop a plan as said in last section in which I will mention now which is my "get up and go" signal in my head whenever I see a child.

My plan is to imagine that a child is a bright revolving red light to an extreme flaming building and that to get out of that area fast before any danger occurs because if I go near the burning building I could get seriously burned or hurt by fire/or caught by police and thrown in jail.

This was his plan as it was written in the client's notebook. He then transferred what he wrote onto a blackboard, and verbally explained the individual steps i.e., (see, say, hear, and do). His plan starts at the first *thought* of a child.

Each client makes up their own plans. Clients take these plans home with them. Other plans involve snapping an elastic band that is worn on the wrist, every time there is a thought of a child. Ammonia tabs can be snapped and held under the nose at the thought of a child also.

STEP 5. Evaluation of the Plan

During the great majority of meetings the group evaluates at least one plan in depth, and at the end of each session each member is reminded to use their plan. Repetition is essential. New habits are reinforced by rituals, such as the RESPECT™ Bow, taken from karate, which gives unconditional respect to everyone. RESPECT, by the group for the individual, reinforces and applauds participation by choice. People motivate themselves by forming beliefs about what they can do, anticipating likely outcomes, setting goals, and planning courses of action (Bandura, 1997).

STEP 6. CHOICE: This Group Gives Me Confidence so I Can Make a Choice

This step involves creating concrete, individual symbolization of the client's reality and past offending behaviors. The exercise is multisensory and involves physical objects to reinforce a client's cognizance of his pedophilia and the steps he has now learned to cope with.

Since most of the group members have unskilled positions, such as garage worker, janitor, cleaner, they have the opportunity to use/bring in tools they have used in their occupations. The goal of the exercise is to use tools that are used and touched on a daily basis, so that the learning is physical, not theoretical. If a client remembers the steps he has taken to solve his problems, then he is empowered to make choices.

The psychotherapist uses the objects to represent various steps of the RESPECT™ System. For example, he may use a broom, a coffee can filled with sand, gravel, broken glass, a dust pan or fireplace shovel, a waste basket, a sink, soap and water. The broom is a tool. The coffee can contents are dumped on the floor by the client. The perpetrator says, "This is a child's pain–sexual abuse." The broom, for example, could be representative of the perpetrator's REALITY; the shovel, his EMPATHY. Together, they forge SELF-ESTEEM that gives confidence and courage to clean up the pain that has been caused by a perpetrator. The group helps the individual on his CHOICE step to use his PLAN to clean up his offense. He will read his plan and explain it. When an individual chooses to participate on the CHOICE step, he gets physically involved in an action. Internalizing the concept of positive choice is the goal. A client asks, "Am I dirty?" Now, he can choose to go to the sink, wash his hands with soap, and return to the group. He will explain to the group what this exercise meant to him and move on to the next step. The message: Past behavior cannot be controlled. Present behavior can. You are not only your past. You are also, now. We cannot control what others think or how they behave toward us, but we can choose to control our own behaviors.

Glasser, W. (1998) writes:

1. The only person whose behavior we can control is our own. In practice, if we are willing to suffer the alternative–no one can make us do what we don't want to do. When we are threatened with punishment, whatever we do we rarely do well.

    When we actually begin to realize that we can control only our own behavior, we immediately start to redefine our personal freedom and find, in many instances, we have much more freedom than we realize.
2. All we can give or get from other people is information. How we deal with that information is our or their choice (pp. 332, 333).

STEP 7. TRUST: This Group Is No Malarkey. Look at Me. I'm on the Trust Step. If I See a Kid, I Just Walk Away

Having reached this step, clients can choose to come to group meetings every other week instead of weekly. After one month they can choose to come every third week for the next three months.

A client on the TRUST step explains to the other group members who are still on the lower steps, what he is experiencing in his community, and how he is using his plan. The group members still on the lower steps see, hear, and experience another member's success. The concept of TRUST has become real and attainable because they have seen it, heard it, and felt it.

Sometimes, members who have completed the RESPECT™ system, come back. If they have not reoffended, they will be able to stay on the TRUST step, but will *own* their new reality, and start the RESPECT™ System from the beginning to solve their new problem. If they have reoffended, they lose TRUST and begin again. Losing the TRUST step is a powerful motivator not to reoffend. By the time group members have completed the TRUST step everyone knows that pedophilia is forever. The perpetrator knows that the RESPECT™ System is only a tool to keep himself and his community safe and the tool is only as good as the commitment of the person using it.

DISCUSSION

The RESPECT™ System was under development at the Lipton Center in Fitchburg, Massachusetts beginning in August of 1988. To date, 24 pedophiles have been treated or are currently in treatment in the program. One group member was incarcerated for refusing to take the first step, REALITY, when he was requested to return to court by his probation officer. Another member was homeless and was incarcerated for reoffending on the day before Christmas, 1995. He has since come out of jail and has not returned to the group. Another individual, on the TRUST step, was accused of indecent exposure to a child; spent 90 days incarcerated, but was found innocent. He is back in the group and remains on the TRUST step. None of the other group members have reoffended. Two individuals who completed the program have requested to attend the group as maintenance therapy, since they report having obsessive thoughts about children, which returned after one and four years out of the program, respectively.

A young person with minimal social assertion skills and limited cognitive and moral judgment skills who comes from a dysfunctional, poverty-burdened family with no dominant adult model for socially responsible behavior may be guided into criminal activities by more cognitively aware, socially assertive, and goal-directed, delinquent peers (Wettstein,1998). Many individuals that have entered the RESPECT™ System were molested at institutions they were placed, by family members and peers, and have learned that adults having sex with children is part of the growing up process. This is why a habilitation model of treatment is advised.

Unquestionably, the success of different modes of therapeutic intervention in the treatment of sex offenders has proved difficult to assess. According to Miner (1997), the best way to test the effectiveness of a given treatment intervention is to identify the elements of the treatment and the desired changes expected as a result of participating in it Outcome studies should then measure the implementation, the realization of its goals, and finally recidivism.

According to Barbaree (1997), the weakness of recidivism studies to date has been their insensitivity to treatment effects, which gives greater validity to non recidivism studies of treatment efficacy.

The RESPECT™ System focus on enhancement of self-esteem is a vitally important process in the treatment of dually diagnosed sex offenders. As Marshall (1996) notes, treatment to be effective should create the right climate in the treatment setting, and expand social interactions, as well as rehearse positive self statements.

Counterresistence

Working with pedophiles within the RESPECT™ system can bring out issues for the therapist, which fit well within the same framework as that described above for the treatment of the pedophile. As a social worker in 1969, just out of college, I am convinced that I can "cure" poverty, or, at the very least, make a difference. I am assigned to investigate situations involving criminally neglected and battered children. In 1972, a 90 day old child, a member of a family I am investigating, dies of malnutrition, dehydration and there is evidence of sexual abuse. As a result of these and other child abuse experiences, I become cynical, judgmental and loath individuals who abuse children, especially pedophiles. I quit the field. In 1985, as a clinician, I began working with dually diagnosed adults, who also have physical handicaps, in a psychiatric day treatment setting. I think I have consciously and clinically removed myself from child abuse issues. The first pedophile, (1988), I began to treat clinically was someone that was already in my treatment for other behavioral problems before his pedophilia surfaced as a clinical problem. The benefit to this reality was I knew him outside of a pedophile context. For this clinician there were two realities–the reality of pedophilia–the reality of judging the pedophile.

The therapist's interference with the therapeutic process, G. Schoenewolf (1993):

> . . . the first and foremost responsibility of psychotherapists is to analyze their own resistance. Once therapists have analyzed and resolved their *own* resistance to their patients, the rest will follow. . . . Moreover, it is my contention that in most cases, therapeutic failures result not from the inability of analysts to analyze and resolve patients' resistance, but from failure to analyze and resolve their own. (Preface)

Schoenewolf further notes:

> In psychotherapy, too, the less one does the better it is. Perhaps the hardest thing for a novice therapist to learn is not to try to cure a patient. The curing takes place of its own accord. The desire to cure a patient–or to do anything to or for a patient–is a counterresistence. (p. 33)

In the first step, REALITY: *You have to own it to change it.* The pedophile has to "own" he has seriously harmed a child–the therapist has to "own" his judgment of the pedophile; separate the person from the offense; and let go of the premise that he is there to "cure pedophilia."

EMPATHY: Schoenewolf (1983) notes:

> Many beginning therapists misunderstand the concept of empathy. They think it means showing the patient that they care, when it actually means being able to put themselves in the patient's shoes. (p. 46)

A client on the EMPATHY Step says:

> I was in her feet. I looked at me. I did not like it.

As a clinician behind the eyes of a dually diagnosed pedophile the question is: What's it like to be a 36 year old male; have the mental age of an 8 year old child with hallucinations, and no impulse control? Add to this scenario an institution where I have been left by parents, who didn't know how to take care of me. I am befriended by a staff, at the age of 10 years, who later has sex with me, and it feels good.

By clinically empathizing with this pedophile I see an entirely different paradigm and a plethora of needs to meet before we even start moving toward a viable clinical solution. I determine there is a need to invest in success to counter-balance consistent societal failure. Also, a necessity for a transitional *action* from problem focus to solution that would begin a forgiving–a letting go of the past–a healing. The clinician will let go of his past judgment of pedophiles to learn and practice objectivity. The pedophile will begin to forgive himself; and the group will begin to honor the good in his existence. We will celebrate the courage to take these steps together and call it SELF-ESTEEM.

Schoenewolf further writes:

> If a therapist can experience the countertransference feelings and objectify them (and not act them out through some kind of resistance), they can be used to understand the patient's transference defenses and identifications; however, if the therapist cannot objectify the countertransference feelings, they will become countertransference resistance's. This, again, points out the importance for therapists to analyze themselves first, and then their patients. (p. 72)

If the therapist is going to continue to treat pedophilia he needs a PLAN. That plan will involve research and joining other sex offender therapists to EVALUATE this plan. For this therapist there were two CHOICES–grow or quit. With two choices we have two steps–reality and choice. Two steps grow to seven steps that spell out RESPECT. The group and I agree: Everybody has problems. All problems are beginnings to solutions. It is better to work toward solutions together. Nobody is better than anybody else. Everybody and every problem deserves our respect.

Schoenewolf observes:

> All progress in group treatment parallels the analyst's discovery of his own inner life as prompted by his or her patients. Ormont writes (1992) viewing group therapy as a learning experience for both therapist and members, he adds, by relying on what goes on in group for our own self understanding, we are best able to help the members. (p. 82)

REFERENCES

Bandura, A., (1997, March). Self-efficacy. *Insights, The Harvard Mental Health Letter, 13*, 4-6.

Barbaree, H., (1997) Evaluating treatment efficacy with sexual offenders: The insensitivity of recidivism studies to treatment effects. *Sexual Abuse: A Journal of Research and Treatment, 9*, 126-127.

Berg, I.K., DeJong, P. (1998). *Interviewing for Solutions.* Albany Brooks/Cole.

Breggin, P.R. (1991). *Toxic Psychiatry.* New York: St. Martin's Press.

Campbell, R., (1989), *Psychiatric Dictionary.* New York: Oxford University Press Inc.

Gardner, H. (1985), *Frames of Mind: The Theory of Multiple Intelligences.* NY: Basic Books, Inc.

Gardner, W.I., & Cole, C.L. (1989). *Self-management approaches.* In E. Cipani (Ed.), *The treatment of severe behavior disorders* (pp. 19-36). Washington, DC: American Association on Mental Retardation.

Gardner, W.I. (1991). Effects of psychological welfarism on durability of behavior disorders in those with mental retardation. *Psychology in Mental Retardation and Developmental Disabilities, 16*, 2-5.

Glasser, W. (1975). *Reality therapy.* New York: Harper & Row.

Glasser, W. (1998). *Choice theory.* New York: HarperCollins.

Goldstein, A.P., & Glick, B. (1987). *Aggression replacement training.* Champaign, IL: Research Press.

Haaven, J., Little, R., & Petre-Miller, D. (1990). *Treating intellectually disabled sex offenders, A model residential program,* Orwell, Vt.: The Safer Society Press.

Hayes, S.C. (1989). *Rule-governed behavior.* New York: Plenum Press.

Laski, F.J. (1992). *Sentencing the offender with mental retardation: Honoring the imperative for immediate punishments and probation.* In R.W. Conley, R. Luckasson, & G.N. Bouthilet (Eds.), The criminal justice system and mental retardation (pp. 137-152). Baltimore: Brookes.

Leberman, R.P., DeRisi, W.J., & Meuser, K.T. (1989). *Social skills training for psychiatric patients.* New York: Pergamon Press.

Marshall, W., (1996). The sexual offender: Monster, victim, or everyman?: *Sexual Abuse: A Journal of Research and Treatment, 8,* 317-335.

McGee, J.J., & Menolascino, F.J. (1992). The evaluation of defendants with mental retardation in the criminal justice system. In R. W. Conley, R. Luckasson, & G.N. Bouthilet (Eds.), *The criminal justice system and mental retardation* (pp. 55-77). Baltimore: Books.

Miner, M., (1997). How can we conduct treatment outcome research?: *Sexual Abuse: A Journal of Research and Treatment, 9*, 108.

Murphy, W.D.., Coleman, E.M., & Haynes, M.R. (1983). Treatment and evaluation issues with the mentally retarded sex offender. In J.G. Greer & I.R. Stuart (Eds.), *The sexual aggressor: Current perspectives on treatment* (pp. 22-41). New York: Van Nostrand Reinhold.

Nightingale, E. (1999). What you ought to be. *Motivational Moments, Insight.* Nightingale-Conant Corp., Niles, IL.

Ormont, L. (1992). *The group therapy experience.* New York: St. Martin's Press.

Rose, C. (1995). *Accelerated learning systems ltd. action guide.* Buckinghamshire, England: Nightingale-Conant Corp.

Scheuermann, T., Stephens, L., Newman, B., & Dyer, B. (1991). *The Man Within.* Nashville Tennessee: Thomas Nelson Inc.

Schoenewolf, G. (1993). *Counterresistence.* Northvale, New Jersey: Jason Aronson Inc.

Wettstein, R.H. (1998) *Treatment of offenders with mental disorders.* New York: Guilford Press.

Wylie, M.S., (1998, November/December). Secret lives. *The Family Therapy Network, Inc. 22,* 39-59.

Index

Academic Medical Center,
    Amsterdam, 19-36
Adolescent female sexual offenders,
    7-8,75-88. *See also* Female
    sexual offenders
Adrenocorticotropic hormone
    (ACTH), 25,29
Aggression
    background and principles, 20-21
    sexual. *See* Sexual aggression
    in women, 22. *See also*
        Female sexual
        offenders
Aggressor, identification with
        (Stockholm syndrome), 30
Anabolic steroids, 23. *See also*
    Androgen-related sexual
    aggression
Analgesia, stress-induced, 30
Androgen-related sexual aggression,
    21-23
Animal experiments, 20-21
Antecedants to treatment, 15-16
Antidepressant drugs, 30

Biomedical mechanisms, 5. *See also*
    Brain abnormalities;
    Neuroendocrinology
Biomedical treatment, defined, 14
Brain abnormalities, 23-24
    magnetic resonance imaging (MRI)
        self-concepts and interpersonal
        perceptions in, 49-56
        self-perceived aggression in
        incarcerated offenders, 37-47
        violent behavior, 57-64
    tumors, 23-24

Brain development, 26-27
Brain tumors. *See also* Brain
    abnormalities
    aggression and, 23-24

Caracas International Conference on
    the Treatment of Sexual
    Offenders (1998), 1-9
Child molesters
    family therapy with, 65-74
    RESPECT 7-step system for, 6,
        89-114. *See also* RESPECT
        7-step system
Competence, professional, 14-15
Computed tomography (CT scan),of
        brain abnormalities, 38-40
Contraceptive studies, male, 22-23
Corticotropin-releasing hormone,
        25-26,29

Dementia, semantic, 45-46
Depression, 30
Development, brain, 26-27
Domestic violence, 22
Dopamine, 29
Dual diagnosis. *See* Mental
        retardation; RESPECT™
        7-step system

FAF Inventory, 49-56
Family involvement, 6-7,65-74
    recidivism and, 70-71
    treatment disposition and, 68-70
Female sexual offenders, 6-7,75-88
    discussion, 83-87
    life stressors and, 81

© 2000 by The Haworth Press, Inc. All rights reserved.

literature review, 76-77
psychological problems in, 80
sexual abuse experienced by, 83,86
sexual health and sexual histories
in, 81-82
study design, 77-79
victim selection by, 83
Frankfurt Scales of Self-Concepts, 49-56

5-Hydroxyindolacetic acid (5-HTA).
See Serotonin

IATSA (international Association for the
Treatment of Sexual Abusers)
establishment of, 3
goals and values of, 3-4
Interactional Anxiety Scale, 42
International Conference on the
Treatment of Sexual
Offenders (1998), 1-9
*Inventory for the Assessment of
Factors of Aggressiveness*
(FAF), 42-43,49-56
Inventory of Interpersonal Problems,
41-42

LHPA axis, 29,30
Limbic system, 25

Magnetic resonance imaging (MRI),
of brain abnormalities
self-concepts and interpersonal
perceptions, 49-56
self-perceived aggression, 37-47
violent behavior, 57-64
Male contraceptive studies, 22-23
Male sexual offenders. *See under*
Sexual offenders
Measures
Frankfurt Scales of Self-Concepts,
49-56

Interactional Anxiety Scale, 42
*Inventory for the Assessment of
Factors of Aggressiveness*
(FAF), 42-43,49-56
*Inventory of Interpersonal
Problems*, 41-42
Memory, 27
Mental retardation, RESPECT™ 7-step
system in, 89-114. *See also*
RESPECT™ 7-step system
(University of) Minnesota School
of Medicine, 1-9,11-17

Neurotransmitters, 27-29
catecholamines, 28
dopamine, 28
serotonin, 28-29
North Carolina Sexual Offender
Treatment Program (SOTP),
65-74

Paraphilias, defined, 12,13-14
Pedophiles, 65-74. *See also* Child
molesters
Pharmacological treatment, 31-32
Physical handicaps, RESPECT™
7-step system in, 89-114. *See
also* RESPECT™ 7-step
system
Positron emission tomography (PET
scan), of brain abnormalities,
38-40
Posttraumatic stress disorder, 30-31
Professional competence, 14-15
Psychological treatment
defined, 14
family therapy, 6,65-74
Psychoneuroendocrinology
background and principles of
aggression studies, 20-21
early brain development and early
stress, 26-27
limbic system, 26
neuroendocrinology of stress
system, 25-26

neurotransmitters, 27-29
pharmacologic interventions, 31
sex differences in stress disorders, 29
(sexual) aggression as maladaptive
    stress response, 24-31
stress-response disorders, 29-31

Recidivism,family involvement and,
    70-71
RESPECT™ 7-step system, 89-114
    counterresistance issues in, 110-112
    description and background, 90-95
    discussion, 109-112
    principles of, 95-99
        accelerated multi-sensory
            learning techniques, 97-98
        rituals, 96-97
        self-efficacy, 98-99
        solution focus, 95-96
    steps of, 99-109
        1. Reality, 101-102
        2. Empathy, 102-103
        3. Self-esteem, 103-104
        4. Plan, 105-107
        5. Evaluation of plan, 107
        6. Choice, 107-108
        7: Trust, 108-109

Selective serononin reuptake inhibitors
    (SSRIs), 30
Semantic dementia, 45-46
Sex differences, in stress disorders, 29
Sex steroids, 29
Sexual abuse, childhood, 83,86
Sexual aggression, 19-36
    anatomical and functional brain
        disorders in, 23-24. *See also*
        Brain abnormalities
    androgen-related, 21-23
    brain abnormalities and, 4-6
    as maladaptive stress response, 4-5,
        24-31. *See also*
        Psychoneuroendocrinology
    early brain development and

early stress, 26-27
limbic system, 26
neuroendocrinology of stress
    system, 25-26
neurotransmitters, 27-29
sex differences in stress
    disorders, 29
stress-response disorders, 29-31
neuroendicrinology of. *See* Brain
    abnormalities;
    Neuroendocrinology
pharmacological interventions in,
    31-32
psychoneuroendocrinology of,
    19-36. *See also*
    Psychoneuroendocrinology
Sexual offenders
defined, 14
female, 75-88
male
    child molesters, 65-74. *See also*
        Child molesters
    as compared with female, 75-88
    MRI studies of brain
        abnormalities, 37-47,49-56,
        57-64
Sexual Offender Treatment Program
    (SOTP), 65-74
Sexual offense, defined, 14
Sexual trauma, 30
Standards of care, 2-3,11-17
    antecedants to treatment, 15-16
    definitions used in, 13-14
    principles of, 16-17
    for professional competence, 14-15
    purpose statement for, 13
Steroids
    anabolic, 23. *See also*
        Androgen-related sexual
        aggression
    sex, 29
Stockholm syndrome, 30
Stress
    early, 26-27
    neonatal, 27
Stress-induced analgesia, 30

Stress response, (sexual) aggression as
    maladaptive, 24-31. *See also
    under* Sexual aggression
Systems approach to treatment, 65-74

Testosterone, 21-23
Trauma, sexual, 30
Treatment
    antecedants to, 15-16
    family therapy, 65-74
    pharmacological, 31-32
    psychological, 65-74
    standards of care for, 11-17
    systems approach to, 65-74
Treatment disposition, family
    involvement and, 68-70
Tumors, aggression and brain, 23-24

University of Minnesota School of
    Medicine, 1-9,11-17

Vienna University School of
    Medicine, 5-6,37-45,49-56,
    57-64
Violence
    brain abnormalities and, 39-40,
    57-64
    domestic, 22
    as maladaptive stress response,
    24-25
Violence ratings/violence scales,
    41-43
Violencia 98 conference, 2